Franz Kafka

Titles in the series Critical Lives present the work of leading cultural figures of the modern period. Each book explores the life of the artist, writer, philosopher or architect in question and relates it to their major works.

Franz Kafka

Sander L. Gilman

REAKTION BOOKS

Published by Reaktion Books Ltd
79 Farringdon Road
London EC1M 3JU, UK

www.reaktionbooks.co.uk

First published 2005

Printed and bound in Great Britain by
Cromwell Press, Trowbridge, Wiltshire

British Library Cataloguing in Publication Data
Gilman, Sander L.
    Franz Kafka. – (Critical lives)
    1. Kafka, Franz, 1883–1924 2. Kafka, Franz, 1883–1924 –
    Criticism and interpretation 3. Novelists, Austrian –
    20th century – Biography
    I. Title
    833.9'12

    ISBN 1 86189 254 3

Contents

Kafka's draft opening of *The Trial*.

Introduction

In many ways Franz Kafka was a typical Jewish male of turn-of-the-century Central Europe – in every way, that is, except for his uncanny ability to capture on paper the uncomfortable sense of alienation he felt. Harold Bloom, in his presentation of *The Western Canon* (1994), is quite right that 'despite all his denials and beautiful evasions, [Kafka] quite simply is Jewish writing.' Yet this is also not quite enough. His ability to express what he felt about his own complex Jewish identity, in a form that was accessible from every direction, made him into the author who most fully captured the sense of alienation, in all of its forms, that haunted the twentieth century. It is said that today there is no literary language in which the adjective 'Kafkaesque', or the adverb 'Kafkaesquely', is not understood. Kafkaesque is eerie, randomly occurring, too real, yet somehow not real enough. More banally, it is defined by the *Oxford English Dictionary* as 'of or relating to the Austrian writer Franz *Kafka* (1883–1924) or his writings; resembling the state of affairs or a state of mind described by Kafka'. It is a word in use for more than 50 years, at least in English. Kafka appears first in English in the early 1930s. By 1947 William Shawn, the editor of the *New Yorker*, then the most read American magazine for intellectuals, could already write of one 'warned, he said, by a Kafka-esque nightmare of blind alleys'. Arthur Koestler, another Habsburg Jew, wrote in 1954 about the curse of Communism (what else?), 'long before the Moscow purges revealed that weird, Kafka-esque pattern to the incredulous world'. Alan Paton in *Ah, but Your Land is Beautiful* (1981) sees apartheid South Africa in just such terms: 'When she brought them in, he understood her apprehensiveness at once. How could she see that they were men of tremendous authority. He had never read Kafka, but if he had he would have recognized them. They wore black suits, and did not smile when they greeted him, or offer to shake hands.' David Lodge understands his world too in Kafka's terms but with a comic turn, as when in *Nice Work* (1988) he has the protagonist 'toiling up the slope from the Falmer railway station, [where he] had the Kafkaesque sensation of walking into an endlessly deep stage set where apparently three-dimensional objects turned out to be painted flats, and reality receded as fast as you pursued it.' In July 1999, well before 9 September 2001, the arrest of one of Osama bin Laden's associates in London was dismissed by his lawyer as a 'Kafkaesque American abuse of power'. All the world registers 'Kafka' as a 'brand name', to be used when evoking the horrors and complexities of the modern world.

Kafka, discovered in the 1920s by the Expressionists, damned by the Nazis in the 1930s and by the Marxists at more or less the same time, was reinvented after World War II by the French Existentialists. They saw in him the father of Angst and the Angst for the father: an Albert Camus before his time. But since then he has been reshaped, rethought, reread, many times. By the 1990s the American poet Kenward Elmslie could mock the world of the Kafkaesque in recounting his own autobiographical path to Kafka:

> From crazy brat reading Krazy Kat
> To Kafkaesque this Kafkaesque that
> Never saw 'action' ransacked my dance act
> Came up with a nance act

How Kafkaesque!

Thus the Kafkaesque works of Franz Kafka are the most read and most contested in 'modern' literature. But the man seems just as Kafkaesque. A long line of biographies has tried to capture the man behind the words. From the first, that of his friend Max Brod, to the more recent biographies of Hartmut Binder, Rotraut Hackermüller, Ronald Hayman, Frederick Robert Karl, Peter Alden Mailloux, Ernst Pawel, Marthe Robert, Klaus Wagenbach, Reiner Stach and Nicholas Murray, each biographer has sought to present a Kafka that made sense in his or her Kafkaesque system. And what is most remarkable about the bountiful interpretations and biographies is that every critic was right and every biographer was right! Kafka turns out to be as much an Expressionist as a Zionist as a mystic as a pre- and post-Communist Czech as an Existentialist as a post-modernist as a post-colonialist as a (whatever he will be next month). Kafka's work and his life seem to lend themselves to infinite readings and finite exploitations. The fact that one can buy marzipan *Ungeheuer Ungeziefer* ('Monstrous Bugs') in Prague (the Kafkaesque equivalent of Salzburg's *Mozartkugeln*) shows that this infinite re-reading of Kafka is not limited to the intellectuals. Even the sweet-makers in Prague have read Kafka's *Metamorphosis*, the story of a man who turns into a bug, and know how to market it. Kafka has become the logo of Czech tourism in the twenty-first century. He reappears in a form very different from that presented during the 1968 'Prague Spring', where he had been the sign of a cultural renewal independent of Soviet domination. Kafka rules!!!! And this is just as true of mass and popular culture, from the film to the illustrated novel to the tourist kiosk in Prague and beyond. It is almost as if Kafka had planned this. It is most Kafkaesque.

Now, it is clear that Kafka did plan all of this very carefully; it is how he planned it that makes the need for this biography most necessary. Kafka was an obsessive who one day suddenly sits down to write 'Das Urteil' ('The Judgment'), which, Mozart-like, flows out of him. It is completely there with all its coolness and distance, with all its engagement and horror. Here is the Kafka as original genius, able to become himself because of his response to his father and sister or mother and, most evidently, to Prague and the world that it embodied. Here is the writer who compensates for his sexual, or at least personal, inadequacies with younger women by writing them such a stream of letters that they are overwhelmed and then quite disappointed, much like the cakes offered in the Prague cafés that looked delicious but tasted like flour paste. Kafka is a psychological 'case' and proof, if we in the West truly need it, that unhappiness, depression and inadequacies are the stuff that makes genius – just like Beethoven.

With Kafka there is a problem. Kafka knew all of the tricks. He understood his Freud, he understood Oedipus as a cultural phenomenon, he read his psychology, and, at least according to his remarks, did not think much of it. Much like the problem of trying to understand the archetypes of Herman Hesse through the lens of his intellectual mentor C. G. Jung, understanding Kafka as a 'case' is complicated. When Kafka sits down to write, he plans carefully and with much forethought; he thinks and edits much even before it comes to his pen. He eliminates any sense of himself as a historical figure. He strips from his fiction and (I would argue) from the letters to friends and lovers (whatever that word means in his vocabulary) all that would identify him in terms of his own perception of the world. Part of this can be seen in the manuscripts themselves, but much of the real editing took place before he ever put pen to paper.

When Kafka looks at Goethe's manuscripts during a visit to Weimar in 1912 he is shocked that Goethe seems never to cross out or rewrite. The poems appear to flow from him, just as Mozart heard the music complete in his head. Kafka was Beethoven, who crossed out, rewrote and eventually could not even hear what he wrote. Kafka's great hulks of abandoned novels, those major texts by which we define him today – the worlds of the stoker, of the trial, and the castle – were the late symphonies, unheard, unread, unfinished.

Kafka's texts, including these fragments, are infinitely readable and interpretable, for every reader, for every critical school, for every age. This does not differ from the work of the deaf Beethoven. There seems to be no 'objective correlative' in them, no 'real' worlds to which they might refer – only a set of words depicting a world that exists beyond his cold, impassionate control. He is not Borges (and Borges is not him): there is no Don Quixote in Kafka's world. But there is Don Quixote and, equally important, Kafka in Borges's world, as he writes of the *Iliad* in a text included in his *Labyrinths* (1970), 'the moving object and the arrow and Achilles are the first Kafkian characters in literature.' All of literature becomes Kafkaesque after Kafka. This means it is infinitely rereadable and inherently uninterpretable because it is so very interpretable. There are no such anchors in the external world in Kafka's writing. He has eliminated them self-consciously and we need serious, historical work to replace them. They shaped or deformed the texts much more than we can imagine.

The worlds of interpretation that Kafka builds into his work are made concrete by readings beginning with the 1930s that turn Kafka into a Jewish mystic, a Marxist prophet, an existentialist priest, into the best of Christians and the worst of Jews. (Sometimes this is hard to fathom, as when John Updike observes that 'Kafka, however unmistakable the ethnic source of his "liveliness" and alienation, avoided Jewish parochialism, and his allegories of pained awareness take upon themselves the entire European – that is to say predominantly Christian – malaise.') Films, poems, short stories and novels 'remember' Kafka, playing the very game that he wanted them to play. Kafka was a passionate reader but an even more passionate filmgoer. His reception was already part of his game.

Jens Peter Müller, 'the most beautiful man of the new century',
according to the novelist Erich Kästner.

1

My Family and my Body as a Curse

It is a frosty, damp early morning in 1917. Passers by look up at an odd sight for central Prague. A young man, stripped to the waist, stands at the open window of his apartment in what had been the Schönborn Palace, doing calisthenics for a full ten minutes. Exercise and repeat, exercise and repeat every evening at 7.30 p.m. The craze for body-building exemplified by the strongman Eugene Sandow (1867–1925) had an exponent in the civil servant Franz Kafka. Exercise, row, swim, ride horses, build your body, transform yourself. Light clothing even in the midst of winter was the litany of the body-builder Jens Peter Müller, who abjured the use of Sandow's (Indian) clubs and spring dumbbells (all sold to eager young men through the post). Müller, on the other hand, sold special sandals and books on sexual hygiene. But both believed that bodily transformation was not only possible but also necessary in order to become a modern man.

Kafka, this young Jewish citizen of multicultural Prague in the first decade of the new twentieth century, shunned the devices but he did body-build compulsively. He fletcherized at every meal. 'Nature will castigate those who don't masticate', said Horace Fletcher (1849–1919). Chew your food 32 times and you will have a healthier body and a happier soul. Franz's father hid behind his newspaper, not wanting to watch his son chew. Franz Kafka exercising in a decaying castle in the middle of Prague, compulsively chewing his food, desiring to control his body. Kafka was not alone in his compulsive chewing. The philosopher and psychologist William James, by then a professor at Harvard, regularly fletcherized.

Slightly under six feet tall (1.82 m) and weighing 133 pounds (61 kg), Kafka was someone whose mother constantly encouraged him to 'eat, eat, my son'. The average Czech man of the time was five foot five to six inches tall and the average Central European Jew was much shorter – five foot. Inordinately thin, compulsively hypochondriac, Kafka's preoccupation with his body was, however, not solely a narcissistic quirk. Sandow, born Friedrich Müller in Prussia, was the ideal male body with whom all young men of the day identified: in 1902, aged 35, he was 5 ft 9 in (1.75 m) tall, weighed 202 lb (91.6 kg) and had a 48 in (121 cm) chest. When Franz Kafka went in 1907 for a physical for his first job at the Assicurazioni Generali Insurance Company, Dr Wilhelm Pollack, the company doctor, described his body in detail:

> His body is thin but delicate [*gracil*]. He is relatively weak. His stride is secure, relaxed. The circumference of his neck is 37 cm. He shows no signs of goiter. His voice is pure and strong. He looks younger than his age. The form and structure of his chest – his breast is raised, his clavicle is drumstickshaped and indented at its ends. He has weak chest muscles. With a deep breath his chest circumference at level of his nipples is 82 cm and on expiration it is 78 cm. Both halves of his chest are equally developed but weak. He takes 16 breaths a minute when resting; and 19 per minute with exercise. The percussion of the right upper lobe of his lung is dull as a result of an earlier rachitic deviation. No anomalies by auscultation; no anomalous sounds.[1]

As with much of his unremarkable life, the banal requirement of such physical examinations is transmuted into a literary trope in Kafka's diaries for July 1914, where 'Bauz, the director of the Progress Insurance Company', informs the unnamed job applicant:

You're tall enough . . . I can see that; but what can you do? Our attendants must be able to do more than lick stamps . . . Your head is shaped peculiarly. Your forehead recedes so. Remarkable . . . Naturally, we can employ only people in good health. Before you are taken on you will have to be examined by a doctor. You are quite well now? Really? Of course, that could be. Speak up a little! Your whispering makes me nervous . . . As long as you're already here, have the doctor examine you now; the attendant will show you the way. But that doesn't mean you will be hired, even if the doctor's opinion is favorable . . . Go along and don't take up any more of my time.[2]

External appearance signals the applicant's mental health or illness and Kafka consciously sees himself always as the victim of such practices. Yet it is clear that the world of this little fable is not simply Kafka's experience recorded but transformed in a way in which writing about it gives Kafka the power to control what seems to be uncontrollable.

Being intrinsically 'sickly' and in need of transformation meant, in Kafka's world, being Jewish. In 1912 the Prague Zionist newspaper *Selbstwehr* (Self-defence), avidly read by Kafka, stated that the Jews must 'shed our heavy stress on intellectual preeminence . . . and our excessive nervousness, a heritage of the ghetto . . . We spend all too much of our time debating, and not enough time in play and gymnastics . . . What makes a man a man is not his mouth, nor his mind, nor yet his morals, but discipline . . . What we need is manliness.' Of course, manliness is healthiness. The Jewish male body was imagined in the time as diseased, deformed, at risk, unmanly. Indeed, Sandow's tradition of body-building was carried into the 1920s by the Polish Jewish strongman Zishe Breitbart (1893–1925), popularly known as the 'Strongest Man in the World'. He bit through iron chains 'as though they were soft pretzels and bent a 7.5-millimetre-thick iron rod like straw', one Berlin reporter wrote at the time. Breitbart appeared before huge Jewish and non-Jewish audiences across Central Europe, frequently in Berlin, Vienna and Prague, and his advertising stressed his Jewish identity, including Jewish iconic images such as the Star of David. Among Jews he was referred to as 'Shimshon hagibor' (Samson strongman) when he appeared flanked by the Zionist flag. He even performed for his Jewish audiences as Bar Kochba, who led the Jewish revolt against Rome between 132 and 135 CE. His body was what Kafka over time wished his own to be: the transformed Jew as hero.

The young Franz Kafka turned his 'physical' deformation into his intellectual calling card. His 'sickly' body becomes the equivalent of his deformed psyche:

> It is certain that a major obstacle to my progress is my physical condition. Nothing can be accomplished with such a body . . . My body is too long for its weakness, it hasn't the least bit of fat to engender a blessed warmth, to preserve an inner fire, no fat on which the spirit could occasionally nourish itself beyond its daily need without damage to the whole. How shall the weak heart that lately has troubled me so often be able to pound the blood through the length of these legs. It would be labor enough to the knees, and from there it can only spill with a senile strength into the cold lower parts of my legs. But now it is already needed up above again, it is being waited for, while it is wasting itself below. Everything is pulled apart throughout the length of my body. What could it accomplish then, when it perhaps wouldn't have enough strength for what I want to achieve even if it were shorter and more compact.[3]

For Kafka his body, including his 'weak heart' and 'mental instability', is a legacy of the two families from which he sprang: the Kafkas and the Löwys. In his vituperative but unsent 'Letter to the Father', part fiction, part autobiography, all construction, written in 1919, he describes himself as:

> a Löwy with a certain Kafka component which, however, is not set in motion by the Kafka will to life, business, and conquest, but by a Löwyish spur that impels more secretly, more diffidently, and in another direction, and which often fails to work entirely. You, on the other hand, [are] a true Kafka in strength, health, appetite, loudness of voice, eloquence, presence of mind, knowledge of human nature, a certain way of doing things on a grand scale.[4]

The Löwys, his maternal family, are the roots of his craziness. Kafka's father, according to the letter of 1919 that Franz never sent him, agreed that his wife's family was tainted by madness, demonstrated by their apparent hereditary predisposition to a whole range of illnesses for which madness was the master category. Kafka's namesake (at least for his Hebrew name Amschel) was his mother's maternal grandfather, Adam (Amschel) Porias (1794–1862), a successful draper who was also 'a very pious and learned man' who 'bathed in the river every day, even in winter'. In evoking this devout if crazed ancestry, Kafka also evokes the problem of his own naming: his Hebrew name is Amschel the Son of his Father, something he can never forget. These begats, in the matrilineal Jewish tradition, return to his mother's mother, who 'died before her time of typhus'. Her death at the age of 29 so affected her own mother (Franz Kafka's great-grandmother) 'that she became melancholy' and committed suicide in 1860. His mother's great-grandfather was a miracle rabbi whose four sons 'all died young', except for his namesake Amschel, who was known as 'Crazy Uncle Nathan', and one daughter, his mother's mother. One of the brothers converted and became a physician. What Kafka does not mention is that his mother, who had 'weeping spells and melancholy', was orphaned at three and was raised with her two brothers and three half-brothers, two of whom, Kafka's uncle Alfred, a director of the Spanish railways, and Rudolf, a bookkeeper in a brewery, were also converts to Catholicism. Family ties and religious identity were closely linked in Kafka's world.

Franz Kafka was born in Prague, in what was then part of the Austro-Hungarian Empire, on 3 July 1883, in the family home at the 'House of the Tower', located at the corner of Maislgasse and Karpfengasse, on the periphery of the Jewish Ghetto. Eight days later he was circumcised and thus became part of the covenant that God had made with Abraham. But this was a different time and a different place and the very notion of a divine covenant took on a very different meaning for the Kafkas. The family moved frequently – at least seven times between Kafka's birth and 1907. Each move was a sign of social and economic improvement but all of the moves were within the confines of Staré Mûsto, Prague's Old Town. As late as 1920 Kafka, living in his parents' apartment in the Oppelthaus Building, turned to his then Hebrew teacher Friedrich Thieberger, gestured toward the window and stated sadly that 'within this little circle my whole life is bounded'. From the window they could see the Old Town Square, his high school, the university and his office. Prague was a complicated city, much like Kafka himself. It was a city, as Kafka noted, with sharp claws. Franz Kafka was a native son but also a stranger, since he was a member of that ancient covenant.

Kafka's grandfathers had been village Jews in rural Bohemia. They primarily spoke Yiddish, the language of Central European Jewry; his father spoke Czech, but when he moved to Prague he opted to identify with the German-speaking community and raised his son to speak German. As the language philosopher and Prague Jew Fritz Mauthner wrote in his 1918 memoirs:

I had to consider not only German but also Czech and Hebrew, as the languages of my 'forefathers' . . . I had the corpses of three languages to drag around with me . . . As a Jew in a bilingual country, just as I possessed no proper native language, I also had no native religion, as the son of a religionless Jewish family. . .'[5]

What changed over time was not only their language but the very meaning that the covenant with God had for them, as Kafka wrote to Max Brod in June 1921:

> And there is a relationship between all this and Jewishness, or more precisely between young Jews and their Jewishness, with the fearful inner predicament of these generations. Psycho-analysis lays stress on the father complex, and many find the concept intellectually fruitful. In this case I prefer another version, where the issue revolves not around the innocent father but around the father's Jewishness. Mostly young Jews who started to write in German wanted to get away from their Jewishness, usually with their father's consent (the vagueness of it was what made it outrageous). They want to get away, but their hind legs still stuck to the fathers' Jewishness, while the forelegs found not firm ground. And the resulting despair served as their inspiration.

But of course there were in Prague two antithetical German-speaking worlds: that of the poet Rainer Maria Rilke (1875–1926), Christian and anti-Semitic to the core, and that of the Kafkas, seen as Jews no matter what their beliefs.

Czechs, too, Catholic, Protestant or Hussite, for the most part looked down on the Jews no matter what their language – and even if they bore a Czech name such as 'Kafka' (blackbird). One needs to note that as part of the civil emancipation of the Jews in the Austro-Hungarian Empire at the close of the eighteenth century, Jews were forced to abandon their traditional naming practices, by which each child took the name of his father as his patronymic, to

Hermann Kafka in the prime of his life. This is the image that Kafka preserves even while his father ages.

have fixed family names like every one else. This made taxation much easier even though a rumour circulated that it was possible to buy 'beautiful' or at least appropriate family names, such as Goldberg (gold mountain) or Seidensticker (silk embroiderer), and that the absence of a small bribe might mean that you could be given rather inappropriate or even offensive names. There is the legend that during the anti-Semitic riots of 1897 Kafka's father's shop was spared because of his 'Czech' name emblazoned on the store window. This was clearly a sum well invested generations before. Kafka's legacy was as much a cultural one as a biological one – and equally conflicted.

Franz's father, Hermann (1852–1931), was a 'self-made man', an importer who operated a store specializing in 'fine goods' for the rising middle-class. His own father, Jakob (1814–1889), had been a kosher butcher in the tiny Czech village of Wossek (now Osek) in rural Bohemia. At the age of ten Hermann had pushed a cart through the rural villages every morning, every season, delivering kosher meat to the local Jews. With his legs covered in frost sores in winter, his life was, at least in his own estimation according to Franz's jaundiced account, that of the 'rags to riches' promise of the rising European middle class who had moved from the countryside to the city. He entered the army at twenty, which fixed his 'German' identity even though his Czech name enabled him to be self-consciously 'on the margin' between the two cultural groups. He came to Prague in the 1870s and opened a store selling haber-dashery and ladies' accessories. Franz describes the Kafkas as brutal, tyrannical and uncultured. Indeed, he credits to them his becoming a vegetarian in 1909 and his lack of musicality:

> Unmusicality is not as clearly a misfortune as you say – in the first place it isn't for me: I inherited it from my predecessors (my paternal grandfather was a butcher in a village near Strakonitz; I have to not eat as much meat as he butchered) and it gives me something to hold on to; being related means a lot to me.'6

Culture and vegetarianism is what the youngest generation of the Kafkas had to recuperate from their past. Indeed when Franz ate at home, he claimed that his father hid his face in the news-paper rather than watching him eat and chew his 'healthy' diet. Kafka's mother, Julie Löwy (1856–1934), came from an orthodox Jewish family whom Kafka considered 'better' (but also crazier) than the Kafkas. Her father had been a cloth-maker in Humpolec in eastern Bohemia.

All of the qualities, however, that Kafka ascribes to the 'mix' between the Löwys and the Kafkas were absent in his much younger sisters: Gabriele 'Elli' (1889–?1942), Valerie 'Valli' (1890–?1942), and Ottilie 'Ottla' (1892–1943). Kafka's brothers Georg (1885–1886) and Heinrich (1887–1888) had both died in infancy and as such made Franz's presence much more valuable in a society that stressed the

Julie Löwy, Kafka's mother, who married Hermann in 1882.

primacy of male children. This is doubly true among Jews for whom only a male child can say the prayer for the dead. Kafka was six years old when Elli was born. As the only male child he saw himself as a quasi-only child ('I am the sad but perfect example'[7]) and felt that he bore the brunt of his father's constant disfavour and his mother's distance. His later siblings had a substantial advantage as 'less attention is paid to them'. As he casts these descriptions in rather Freudian terms, terms that he knew well, we cannot know whether his father was totally demanding and his mother totally subservient to him. All we can know is that Kafka, when he sits down to write about them as an adult, finds in psycho-analysis an appropriate, cutting-edge language with which to cast the image of his parents. I am reminded that 'the fathers have eaten sour grapes and the children's teeth are set on edge' (Ezekiel 18:2) was written well before Freud and Kafka.

For Kafka psychoanalysis is closely tied to his Jewish identity, for good or for ill. In the section of his unpublished papers labelled the 'marriage-notebook' he writes that it 'is not a pleasure to deal with psychoanalysis and I stay far away from it, but it is certainly manifest in this generation. Judaism has always brought forth its sorrows and pleasures with the necessary "Rashi-commentary", so too in this case.' Rashi (Rabbi Shlomo Yitzchaki; 1040–1105 CE) was the outstanding Jewish Biblical commentator of the Middle Ages and Freud seemed to be his contemporary parallel on things Jewish – at least from Kafka's perspective.

Kafka's home life was as the privileged child of a newly bourgeois family. He was educated in the state schools of Prague, beginning

The house in which Franz Kafka was born on 5 July 1885. It stood at the corner of the Karpfengasse and the Maiselgasse (earlier called the 'Enge Gasse' – the narrow street). The old Jewish ghetto was completely transformed during his youth into a 'modern' if still very Jewish part of the city.

Kafka aged five in a studio portrait with a stuffed sheep. One of the fantasies about Jews and urban life was that they had to get back to the soil.

with the heavily Jewish Deutsche Volks- und Bürgerschule (State Grammar School) at the Fleischmarkt (1889–93). Hermann chose a German-language school rather than a Czech one as he wished his family to function within the language of political authority. Ninety per cent of Prague Jews made the same choice. The school was within easy walking distance of the family's then apartment in the Minuta House on the Kleiner Ring. Yet each day he was walked to school by the family's cook and general factotum, a Czech woman whom he felt tormented him. Kafka's account of these trips to school and the complicated sense of the servant's power over his life runs parallel to Sigmund Freud's accounts of how his nursemaid took him to church in Vienna when he too was a small child. The 'truth' of such accounts of the treatment of small Jewish children by their powerless yet 'superior' Christian servants can only be speculated upon. Hermann Kafka referred to his Czech employees as the 'paid enemies'. Yet the sense of the adults (both Kafka and Freud) was that they were in the thrall of their maids, much as they were in the power of their fathers. Despite the fear generated on the way to school, the pair made it each day just as the bell rang. Young Kafka was a 'modest, quiet, good pupil', even though each day during the break there were pitched battles between the 'German' (read: Jewish) children and the Czech children at the grammar school next door. Being quiet meant staying out of harm's way. Kafka's later friend, the novelist Oskar Baum, was blinded in such a playground confrontation.

At ten years old Franz Kafka entered the famed Altstädter Staatsgymnasium (State High School), and studied there from 1893 to 1901. It was an exacting German-language public high school for the academic élite. Here, as in his primary school, a large minority of his fellow students were middle-class Jews. The Jews were emancipated in Bohemia but were still socially isolated and self-isolating: the pressure of anti-Semitism, with the ghetto only three generations prior, was still reflected in social practice. Hermann chose this school with its emphasis on 'classical' learning, rather than the new-fangled ideas about sciences and modern languages, on account of the social advantage it would give his son: Latin and Greek remained the basis for advancement much as the writing of classical Chinese poetry was the key to advancement in the Imperial Court. Only in such an environment is something economically useless seen as proof of the absence of any need to learn a 'trade'.

At high school he met Hugo Bergmann (later spelled Bergman), whose friendship continued throughout his life. Bergmann became a convinced Zionist after reading the 1897 'Basel' Programme in which the Viennese journalist Theodor Herzl called for the

Kafka aged ten with his sisters Valli (left) and Elli (right).

Kafka's high school class picture of 1898. He is in the upper-most row, second from the left; his closest friends: Hugo Bergmann, the Zionist, is in the third row from top, outer most left; Ewald Felix Příbram, the socialist, is in the third row from the top, outer most right.

establishment of a Jewish state; Kafka became a socialist. 'We both experienced the thrill of nonconformity', Bergmann noted decades later. Indeed, when in 1899 the first meeting of the Zionists was held in Prague it was disrupted by Jewish socialists and Czech nationalists who saw the Zionist project as antithetical to their own universal or particular goals. The role of Jews, including Victor Adler, Otto Bauer and Julius Tandler in creating Austro-Hungarian Social Democracy, was seen by many as a socially permissible means of fleeing the stigma of their own Jewish identity. No matter how universal their rhetoric they were regularly denounced as 'red Jews'. It is also the case that some young Jews, such as Manès Sperber, saw socialism as an extension of their Jewish identity and were pleased simultaneously to be socialists and members of Zionist organizations.

Hugo Bergmann remained one of Kafka's strongest connections to the Jewish world. Bergmann joined the Zionist student association Bar Kochba (the role that the strongman Zishe Breitbart would later portray) in 1901. In a letter to Kafka the following year, explaining his commitment to Zionism, he observed that Franz could reach toward the sun and that his dreams spanned the heavens. Bergmann, however, felt that he never dreamt enough and that his own Zionism was a substantial piece of egotism. Bergmann's Zionism was 'spiritual' or 'cultural' Zionism that stressed the intellectual aspects of Jewish peoplehood, including the learning of Hebrew (and Yiddish). The students' task was the 'realization of Judaism' in recapturing the continuity in Jewry that they felt had been ruptured by Jewish acculturation in Western Europe. Yet unlike Bergmann, Kafka always felt himself on the edge of failure no matter how excellently he did: or at least that is how he remembered his school years. Writing to his father in 1919 he sensed that the more he succeeded 'the worse the final outcome would inevitably be'. His focus came more and more to be on his reading and his experiments with writing. He could rattle off the name of any popular author of the day upon hearing the title of his (or her) work. His socialism was equally theoretical, barring any real involvement in the confrontations of the day. As late as 1918 he imagines a new socialist welfare state, a 'brotherhood of poor workers', where working bachelors (as in the Shaker community) would be celibate and use their earnings to help the underprivileged.

Kafka's relationship to religious practice was just as distanced, as was his sense of attachment to a Jewish 'peoplehood'. Even though only seven per cent of Prague's population in 1900 was Jewish, or just over 25,000 Jews, Kafka's world consisted almost exclusively of Jews. Bar mitzvahed at thirteen on 18 June 1896, his relationship to his Jewish education was unengaged. His memory of it was that he had to learn two speeches by heart, one to be delivered in the synagogue and one at home. And that he received many presents. It was a ridiculous exercise, something like passing an examination at school, according to Franz. Indeed, the invitation printed in the name of his father invited the guests to his son's 'confirmation'. The event took place in the early Baroque, German-language Zigeuner Synagogue, which was established in the Jewish Ghetto in about 1613 by Solomon Salkid-Zigeuner and which Franz's father had joined after leaving the Czech-language synagogue in the Heinrichgasse. The building was destroyed by fire and rebuilt several times during its lifetime. But it was there in 1883 that the radical reform services with a choir were introduced. Jews seemed, in Kafka's jaundiced view, to desire to look and act 'like everyone else'.

His parents had abandoned the ritual dietary practices of Orthodoxy; Franz eventually turned to other rituals of food and eating, such as vegetarianism and fletcherization. Indeed even Kafka's refusal to drink alcohol in a culture of beer drinkers (the names Pilsen and Budweiser still resonate) can be understood as a response to the charge lodged time and again against Eastern Jews that they had ritualized drunkenness in celebrations such as Purim. As opposed to the commonly held belief among Jews that only *goyim* (non-Jews) were drunks, there is a long-standing Enlightenment

Jakob Kafka (1814–1889) and his wife Franziska (1816–1880/90). He was the kosher butcher whose slaughtering Kafka imagined he was answering through his vegetarianism.

image of Eastern Jews as inebriates. Things ritually Jewish bored him as he 'yawned and dozed through the many hours' in the synagogue imagining the scroll of the Law as 'just the same old dolls with no heads'. In 1906 the synagogue was torn down for civic improvement, almost a metaphor for Kafka's sense of his Jewish identity at the time. Modernity replaced religion: in 1893 the city council had ordered the ghetto in the Old Town to be 'cleaned up' as it no longer reflected well on a city that had electric trams (from 1891) and telephones (from 1895).

Kafka barely learned enough Hebrew to read the blessings and his portion the day he was confirmed. He was a Jew whose identification with ritual was limited if not non-existent. On 8 January 1914 he was to write in his diary: 'What have I in common with Jews? I have hardly anything in common with myself and should stand very quietly in a corner, content that I can breathe.'[8] Kafka's father, raised in a village defined by Orthodox Judaism, had always demanded that Franz be devout, but at the same time he rarely went to synagogue himself. Religion, for Hermann, had always been a matter of concrete reality. If society saw him as a moral person, then he could consider himself reasonably devout, and there was no reason to bother with those Jewish practices that made him too visible. No ritual head covering or unkempt side locks and beard; no attention to consuming the flesh of ritually slaughtered animals nor to the separation of meat and milk at the table; no attention to the Sabbath as a day to refrain from all work. He attended synagogue for the High Holidays and on the occasion of weddings and funerals. For him that was sufficient given his upbringing in a Jewish culture that had permeated every moment of his young life.

Franz did not grow up in a world where religion and life were inextricably bound. He held a different view. Religion was something separate from reality, and if the rules of heaven were ever applied to earth they would have to be followed painfully to the letter, as if one were balancing an equation. Naturally, Kafka saw his father's ambivalence toward the synagogue as a grave hypocrisy, and from early on he considered himself a religious sceptic. He argued with friends over the mechanistic nature of God as the divine Watchmaker, and soon devoured Baruch Spinoza, Friedrich Nietzsche (whose cult had just begun), and that apostle of the modern, Charles Darwin, as well as his German follower Ernst Haeckel. But he used these readings also for the purposes of youth. He read Nietzsche to his first would-be girlfriend, Selma Kohn, whose family shared a summerhouse outside Prague in the town of Roztoky on the Vltava with the Kafkas in 1900. The seventeen-year-old used his intellect to impress the young girl, reading to her from Nietzsche's works. Ideas can have a pragmatic function in the process of seduction; this was something he learned early and never forgot.

Through his consumption of such books Kafka rejected both capitalism and religion as a teenager – declaring himself to be a socialist and an atheist. But more importantly, although he identified strongly with Czech political and cultural aspirations, his identification with German culture kept even these sympathies subdued. The great 'cultural wars' in Prague in the nineteenth century, which regularly manifested themselves in street riots, were between the Czech and the German speakers. By the time Kafka attended university there was a Czech and a German theatre, university, and virtually everything else in Prague. Language determined identity – or so Kafka hoped. You could change your language (his father was living proof of that), but you could not change your nationality or race. Unlike Jews in Vienna, those in Prague rarely converted or intermarried, but they did shift their linguistic allegiance. Kafka spoke German as his first language but spoke Czech well enough to read and write complex texts. His was a secular world, but one in which the 'Jewish Problem' (always capitalized) was on the front page of the newspapers with the appearance of daily accusations of the 'blood libel', that Jews murdered Christians to use their blood in religious rituals.

The 'Jewish Problem' was a political issue in the struggle for Czech independence. The Czechs were struggling for some form of cultural autonomy (or even pan-Slavic independence) in a 'joint monarchy' where German and Hungarian were the official languages but where dozens of other languages were spoken. Anti-Semitism was part of this struggle as a weapon used by all sides, from the Austrian Imperial (Karl Lueger was regularly re-elected as mayor of Vienna on an explicitly anti-Semitic platform, even though the Emperor detested him) to the various nationalistic splinter groups (including the Czechs). Yet the spokesperson for Czech autonomy, Tomáš Masaryk (1850–1937), later the first president of the independent Czechoslovakia, came out on the side of including the Jews in the Czech body politic when he defended Leopold Hilsner, a shoemaker's apprentice, against a charge of having ritually murdered the nineteen-year-old Christian seamstress Agnes Hruza in 1899. Masaryk urged a retrial after a first conviction, but Hilsner was convicted again in 1900 and served eighteen years before, like Alfred Dreyfus, being pardoned. The 'Jewish Problem' determined what school you went to – remember Kafka's high school was heavily Jewish – and whether you were admitted to University, since there was a *de facto* limit on the number of Jews. By 1891 the dangers confronting Jews in Prague were made manifest with the excess of the so-called 'December Storm' riots that began as attacks on 'German' institutions and ended with attacks on the Jews. They were certainly the most visible minority even in their attempted invisibility.

In other words, for Kafka and his contemporaries, being Jewish at the end of the nineteenth century was an ideological or even a racial category – not necessarily a religious one. Indeed, Kafka's maturation as a secular Jew paralleled the growth of Zionism, the secular, political answer to ubiquitous anti-Semitism in Central and Western Europe – a politics that demanded a new Jewish, but secular, nation for a stateless people. Franz Kafka begins by rejecting the compromises that the reformers, both religious and social, made to traditional Judaism and ends his life strongly identifying with the potential of cultural Zionism as a force of cultural renewal and transformation.

Kafka's social maturation as a young Jewish man also had a private side. His schoolmate Hugo Hecht noted that in school Kafka was 'always very pure' and did not speculate with his friends about the dirty little secrets that shape most adolescent boy's fantasies and dreams. His father, when Franz asked about 'such things', suggested that he learn by doing: go to a whore. Kafka was repelled by this suggestion of the 'filthiest thing possible'. Thus his friends in high school decided that Kafka was ill informed about the 'facts of life' and undertook his enlightenment. One was Hecht, who later became a syphilologist, and the other was an unnamed friend who, according to a letter to his sister Elli in autumn 1921, was destroyed by sex: 'syphilis maimed [him] years ago beyond recognition'. Sex remained 'tainted' for Kafka, as it was for virtually all of his middle-class male contemporaries. This was the age of the moral panic about syphilis. Sex was associated with disease and with fear. Whatever else Kafka sensed about his body, he knew that it was unstable, at risk, profoundly in danger. Sex provided yet one more risk in his world, which was frightening precisely because it threatened his body.

By the time Kafka attended Prague's German-language Ferdinand-Karls University for eight semesters, beginning in November 1901, he was moving in a typical trajectory for secularized Jews in Central Europe. From the rural or ghetto environment of the grandparents to the small manufacturer or shopkeeper of the parents to the status of the professional: Freud, Einstein, Kafka and thousands of others followed this upwardly mobile trajectory. The University was the engine for that final stage of Jewish social mobility. The struggle over admittance of Jews to the various faculties (colleges) of the universities was ongoing. It was only in the 1860s that Jewish students were regularly admitted to the medical faculty in Vienna and then only if they agreed to have only Jewish patients. The Prague university had split into a German and a Czech section in 1882, the year before Kafka was born. There were clear limits to the number of Jews who could be admitted to any one of the faculties, whether German- or Czech-speaking.

Kafka decided initially to become a chemist, since there were said to be jobs for Jews in the chemical industry, but he quickly detested the physical nature of laboratory work. (One is reminded that Primo Levi [1919–1987] maintained his fascination with chemistry, earning his doctorate in 1942 at Turin. This profession saved his life when he was sent to Auschwitz and could work as a chemist: 'I write because I am a chemist. My trade has provided my raw

The life of a bachelor: Kafka's bachelor uncle Dr Siegfried Löwy with four young women, including Kafka's sister Ottla (at the left), on his motorcycle. He was the 'country doctor' whose intervention at the close of Kafka's life was so very vital.

material, the nucleus to which things join . . . Chemistry is a struggle with matter, a masterpiece of rationality, an existential parable . . . Chemistry teaches vigilance combined with reason.') Kafka's friend and fellow chemist-in-waiting Hugo Bergmann stated that Kafka had abandoned the study of chemistry 'because our hands were too clumsy to cope with the glassware'. It was always his body that seemed to betray young Franz. After two weeks he switched to law as a profession that would enable him to earn a living. Bergmann remained in the laboratory of Professor Goldschmied, a converted Jew (which is how a Jew could receive a professorship in Prague), for another year.

By the next semester Kafka was also attending lectures in German literature, which, as it was taught in Prague by August Sauer, stressed the racial determinism of German 'tribal' culture that would have excluded him and all Jews. Kafka joined the

Reading- and Lecture Hall for German Students (*Lesehalle*), a heavily Jewish discussion group, to engage in the intellectual world of letters. This organization attracted the majority of Jews, indeed rather more than joined the Zionist Bar Kochba society. Eventually in 1904 Kafka became the secretary of the Literature and Art section. He had been writing even in high school, if only for his own amusement. In his diary of 19 January 1911 he describes his output of hundreds of pages, including a novel about two brothers, one of whom goes to prison and the other escapes to a fabled America. It was not the America of history that fascinated him but that of German myth, just as it did his older contemporary Karl May (1842–1912), whose novels about mythic America, such as the three volumes of *Winnetou* (1893–1910), paralleled Kafka's own later work and shaped the German image of America to this day. Kafka destroyed all of this once his uncle read a page of the novel and dismissed it as 'the usual stuff'. Childish aspirations towards thinking of himself as a writer ('I did it mostly out of vanity, and by shifting the paper about on the tablecloth, tapping with my pencil, looking around under the lamp, wanted to tempt someone to take what I had written from me, look at it, and admire me.') gave way to a sense of writing as not pursuing the 'usual stuff'. Now writing became more than an avocation – it was a sign that he could belong to a world of culture that wished to exclude him because he was a Jew. But the pressure on him, from his family and his world, was that he also had to be able to function economically.

Kafka dedicated himself full-time to the study of law, which he said he picked because it would not interfere with his creative life. But the study of law in Prague had shifted shortly before Kafka arrived from the rote memorization of legal codes to the study of how the 'law' constructed worlds of meaning, using the cutting-edge biological sciences as the basis for law. Among his teachers was the criminologist Hans Gross, who taught that racial typologies were one of the best indicators of real or potential criminality.

He was particularly fascinated with the Jewish body as revealing the true nature of Jewish difference. Kafka studied with him for three semesters. He also studied with Horaz Krasnopolski, perhaps the most conservative figure at the law school.

Franz's cousin, Bruno Kafka (1881–1931), served as Krasnopolski's 'assistant' and worked his way up the academic ladder, eventually serving as the *Rektor* (President) of the university. When Kafka joined the *Lesehalle*, he found Bruno a prominent member, even reading a paper in Franz's section of literature. Of course, the study of literature, central to European notions of education (*Bildung*), provided a cultural veneer for the bourgeoisie, especially those Jews now entering the middle class for the first time. It enabled them to sound 'like every one else'. But it was not a 'serious' occupation, merely the amassing of cultural capital. Like his teacher, Bruno was strongly German nationalist and was involved in some of the violent confrontations with Czech students when he was a law student. Kafka not only looked down on his politics but also on his attitude toward literature as well as his choice of profession – the law.

Studying law is oddly closely associated with Kafka's sense of his first initiation into the 'mysteries' of the body. When Kafka was twenty and studying for the State examinations after his university studies, he found himself memorizing 'disgusting Roman law' while walking the streets of Prague. He saw a 'shop girl' through a window and, according to a much later letter to Milena Jesenská in 1920, arranged an assignation. The experience was much less awful than he had imagined: 'I was in fact happy, but happy at finally having some peace from my ever-complaining body; happy, above all, that the whole experience hadn't been filthier and more disgusting.' His eventual response to this unnamed woman was disgust and 'she had become my bitter enemy', perhaps because she showed him that his anxieties about his body could be suspended. He concentrated on a misplaced gesture and a rudely spoken word to explain his seeing her as his enemy (as his father

Kafka and the waitress Hansi Julie Szokoll in 1906. She was one of his numerous working-class conquests.

had called his Czech employees). In truth Kafka saw his sexuality in terms of his sexual difference encompassed in the reality of his own circumcised penis. Sexuality, he recounts, 'had in it something of the eternal Jew, being senselessly drawn, wandering senselessly through a senselessly obscene world.'[9] But without these associations he could never be Kafka.

At the university Kafka met another student, a year younger than him, at the Reading and Lecture Hall for German Students after he read a paper on Nietzsche in October 1902. Max Brod (1884–1968) was already a writer of some note and had his own literary circle. His talk, in which he dismissed Nietzsche as a fraud, engaged Kafka, who had already learned the value of Nietzsche as a means of both enlightenment and to seduction in his own life. Brod came from a much higher social class in Prague, having attended, as did the Jewish poet Franz Werfel, the Catholic Piarist School of the Heilige Kreuzkirche along with Rilke. The two would become intimate friends for the rest of their lives. The irony is that the tall, stylish, ever-youthful Kafka, dressed in elegant blue suits, was the handsome one of the pair; Brod was pigeon-breasted and hunchbacked, his huge head out of proportion to his body. Kafka, however, sees him as the epitome of health as opposed to his own 'self-enamored hypochondria'.[10] Even at the end of his life, he writes to Brod admiring how he had come to terms with his disability: Kafka could not even come to terms with his earlier health.[11]

In June 1906 Kafka graduated with his doctorate in law, a guarantee of how he could earn his living without impinging on his true love, the cultural world that he and his friends were joining. And yet Kafka never left the world of work until he was truly too ill to fulfil its claims on him. Work, a job, provided a structure (like his family) that he needed to have, if just to rebel against. Of course, he never rebelled as radically as Otto, his teacher Hans Gross's son, whom his father committed to an asylum because of his radical, psychoanalytically inspired actions, such as providing his patients with the means to commit suicide: but it was just enough, and in his writing, to play at rebellion. Kafka knew and admired the work of the anarchist and psychoanalyst Otto Gross, having met him in July 1917; he committed suicide in 1920. Kafka's 'exile' was self-imposed when in 1903 he went for the first time for a 'rest cure' at a sanatorium in Dresden, 'where you drink air instead of beer and bathe in air instead of water'. He left, as he wrote to his friend Oskar Pollak, healthier and stronger and able to speak with women.

For Kafka had a lively and engaged circle of friends, all of whom saw themselves as the next generation to dominate German culture. In addition to Bergmann, Pollak and especially Brod, this group was part of the extended German-speaking literary world of Prague, most of whom were Jews: the blind novelist Oskar Baum, Johannes Urzidil, Robert and Felix Weltsch, all of whom wrote about their friend Kafka, the syphilitic and half-mad Paul Leppin and Hans Egon Kisch, the German-language inventor of modern muck-raking journalism, as well as his brother Paul. To their ranks

Kafka at the time of his graduation from the faculty of law in 1906.

came writers such as the German Jew Carl Einstein, whose mono-
graph on African sculpture, *Negerplastik* (1915), began a modernist
fascination with the 'primitive', and Gustav Meyrink, the non-
Jewish author of the most famous of all novels about Jewish Prague,
Der Golem (1915). Meyrink was a favourite writer of Max Brod;
Kafka found him 'farfetched and much too blatant. [Kafka] rejected

anything that seemed contrived for effect, intellectual, synthetic'. In other words, too Prague. Unlike the view in the German department at the Charles University, these young Jews – as almost all of them were – saw themselves as the next best hope for German culture, not only in Prague but also in Central Europe. Between 1902 and 1904 Kafka had begun to write the 'Description of a Struggle', the surreal account of, among other things, a conflict between a very thin and a very fat man. It is written in a language quite unlike the overblown and very popular novels of Meyrink. Cool, distant, descriptive rather than evocative, shorn of the excesses not only of Prague writers of his time but of the entire *fin de siècle* love of verbal ornament, Kafka ironically turned to a seemingly transparent language that hid much more than it revealed.

Up the street from the Sixt House, where Kafka had lived as a child from 1888/9, was the Unicorn Apothecary building, adorned on its façade with a sculpture of a child with a unicorn. Here Kafka, often accompanied by Brod and Werfel, attended Prague's only German-language literary salon, which was hosted by the arts patron Berta Fanta, one of the first women to attend the Prague University and whose husband owned the pharmacy downstairs. In 1911 Albert Einstein was also a salon regular during the year he spent 'in exile' as a young physics professor in Prague. At the salon the work of the banned former priest Franz Brentano (1838–1917), with whom Sigmund Freud had also studied in Vienna, was hotly discussed. Brentano provided an empirical and scientific foundation to both philosophy and psychology through his doctrine of intentionality, developing a theory that saw the fundamental acts of one's mental processes, sensations, as linked to consciousness. Brentano's importance for late nineteenth- and early twentieth-century thinkers lay as much, however, in his anti-authoritarian stance as in his philosophy. He became the philosopher of choice for many in Kafka's salon. Eventually he abandoned Fanta's salon because of its unbridled pretentiousness. Kafka moved his allegiance to the Prague Café Arco (among the so-called Arconauts). Here, in addition to intellectual exchange, the circle would regularly adjourn to one of the neighbourhood bordellos, where Kafka, no longer shy and distant, regularly engaged with young women such as the 'twenty-three-year-old girl who provided me with a miracle of a Sunday'.[12] He would sit with his friends, including Max Brod, in local bars such as the Trocadero and the Eldorado, not drinking alcohol but inspecting the available women. With all of his anxieties about sex, with his father's admonition to visit the whores filed away as an example of his crudeness, Kafka can still write that 'I passed by the brothel as though past the house of a beloved.'[13] At least in the brothel there was no anxiety about rejection, even if there was a substantial fear of infection.

Life at the university was demanding and Kafka did what virtually everyone in his generation did when exhausted. He went to a sanatorium for a rest cure. In 1905 he stayed in one run by Ludwig Schweinburg at Zuckmantel (now Zlaté Hory) in Silesia. There he met yet another unnamed 'love'. She was 'a woman, and I was a boy . . . sick in every sense conceivable.' Kafka devoted his time in such sanatoria to seduction. Indeed he writes to Brod in autumn 1905 that he comes there 'to mingle with people and womenfolk'. Illness and desire are self-consciously linked throughout his life, but at this point he was still playing with illness, a use of hypochondria as a means of seduction. That autumn Kafka took his written examinations at the law school, barely passing them, indeed so anxious about them that he contemplates asking for a medical postponement. He received his law degree from the Dean, Alfred Weber, Max Weber's equally renowned sociologist brother, on 18 June 1906. He managed a pass of three out of five votes deeming his performance acceptable.

From the beginning of April to the beginning of October 1906 he served an apprenticeship (*Advokaturs-Concipient*) at the law office of the (unrelated) Richard Löwy. He then spent a year as a 'law probationer' at the Prague Courts. He received an official clearance from the police, which testified to Kafka's being 'unmarried, of Jewish faith and good behaviour'. His earlier interest in socialist thought had not marked his scrupulously clean, middle-class record. He began to sense that law, as a 'calling', would not be his career: he writes on 9 March 1914 in his diary that in no way could he be seen as 'an Austrian lawyer, which, speaking seriously, I of course am not.' In the summer of 1907 he was in Triebsch (now Trebusin), swimming and sunbathing with a nineteen-year-old language student, Hedwig Therese Weiler, whose 'plump little legs' feature in his dreams. After she returned to Vienna and he to Prague he bombarded her with letters over the next two years, trying to get her to visit him. Kafka's world of work was much less engaging – or at least he thought so. He was able to get his first job through his well-connected uncle Alfred Löwy, who lived in Madrid.

The job at the Trieste based Assicurazioni Generali Insurance Company was mindless, boring, very time-intensive – and, needless to say, badly paid. The office, however, was an easy walk from the new Kafka family home in an apartment building in the Niklasstrasse, built over the ruins of the now redeveloped Jewish ghetto. He hoped that the position would lead to something exciting – perhaps foreign travel (at least to Trieste). This did not happen and his desire to write became stymied. Every evening he would meet Max Brod and indulge in the pleasures of Prague at night. He stuck at the job for a year.

Alienated by the work, in May 1908 he attended a course at the Prague Business Institute for Workers' Insurance and passed the examination that allowed him to take a position at the semi-national Workers' Accident Insurance Institute for the Kingdom of Bohemia. This was funded by the employers but run as a quasi-state agency. He was only the second Jew hired: 'the second, last, crumbling Jew'. As with his first job, the new position came through the intervention

of the father of his schoolfriend Ewald Felix Příbram. It was only
once he had the job that he quit his position at Assicurazioni
Generali in July 1908, claiming 'nervousness and cardiac excitability'.
But this was a lie, as he stated decades later in his unsent letter to
his father. His father, he claimed, even in his decline and suffering
a major heart disease, frightened him as did his employer:

> you gradually began to terrify me on all sides . . . the way you
> treated the staff. I don't know, perhaps it was the same in most
> businesses (in the Assicurazioni Generali, for instance, in my
> time it was really similar, and the explanation I gave the director
> for my resignation was, though not strictly in accordance with
> the truth, still not entirely a lie: my not being able to bear the
> cursing and swearing, which incidentally had not actually been
> directed at me; it was something to which I had become too
> painfully sensitive from home).[14]

The actual reason, of course, had nothing to do with his illness or
his father, but the fact that he found a better, less stressful job. On
30 July 1908 he began his new job and found the position much
more conducive, given the shorter hours, to his central goal of
becoming a writer.

At the Workers' Accident Insurance Institute for the Kingdom
of Bohemia Franz Kafka became a consummate professional,
respected as a specialist in accident prevention in workmen's
compensation suits. Since he spoke elegant Czech, he had a strong
relationship with his non-German colleagues, who were impressed
by his 'elegant literary Czech, always with little pauses and the
utmost concentration'. Mandatory compensation for industrial
accidents had been introduced in 1887. The year he was hired the
Institute was reformed with the replacement of its director by
Robert Marschner, whom the newly employed Kafka was designated
to welcome officially. Kafka wrote several sections of the annual

clockwise: Kafka at 27, Elli at 21, Ottla at 18 and Valli at 20.

report for 1910 concerning the need for insurance to protect construction workers' earnings and families in the event of injury. He moved up through the ranks with a certain regularity: in 1908 he was a 'substitute civil servant', in 1910 a regular office worker, in 1913 a vice-secretary, in 1920 secretary, and in 1922 senior secretary.

His superiors saw him as 'an eminently hardworking employee endowed with exceptional talent and devotion to duty', as one of his evaluations reads. His pay rises for this position were generous and very much in line with what senior civil servants earn today.

Kafka constantly asked for leaves of absence owing to bouts of nervousness and exhaustion. But it was exhaustion not from the intellectual life at work, as he notes in February 1911, but from the 'horrible double life' he was leading, 'from which madness probably offers the only way out'. His working day was, however, not at fault. He walked the few blocks from his family's apartment in the Niklasstrasse to arrive at work at 8 a.m. and returned there at 2 p.m., with a substantial mid-morning pause. Family and writing could be escaped through his work, where he can 'peacefully live', but not the office itself, which wore on him just as badly as his home life. Social interaction seems to have been the cause of his deep unhappiness, until one realizes that at the same time he had a lively, engaged, social and intellectual life with the male writers and shop-girls of Prague. In the office he was treated, at least at the beginning, as the 'office baby' because of his eternally youthful appearance; at home he remained the perpetual child of his demanding father. Illness, madness, hypochondria was the only escape from his pedestrian life – except of course when he was with his circle of admirers and friends. After 1919 his office became part of the Czechoslovak government: as he noted, he went from being one of two Jews in the Imperial, German-language office to being the only German in the Czech-speaking office. His bilingualism was always part of his identity, even if his Czech was certainly much shakier than his German.

In this job Kafka's strong social conscience, manifested by his 'socialist' interests as a student, had real results. It was his duty to examine and explain industrial accidents. He looked at how hands and fingers were caught in machinery. He studied trauma and understood the relationship between physical trauma and psycho-

The Aeroplanes at Brescia: Louis Blériot having just crossed the English Channel flies past the assembled audience, among whom was Kafka.

logical states. It was in the world of insurance, decades before, that the 'hysteria' of patients physically unhurt after a train crash but unable to move was first reported as an illness. Kafka knew his Freud, including the claim based on this model of 'railroad spine' that it was the traumatic actions of the fathers that resulted in the illnesses of Freud's female hysterics. Kafka's reports were full of the struggle of the individual in light of the rise of time-motion studies and the most modern of technological innovations.

Machinery fascinated him. In 1909 municipal authorities built an airfield at Brescia in northern Italy and invited leading pilots to compete on it. The show attracted thousands of spectators (among them Giacomo Puccini and Gabriele d'Annunzio) and reporters, including Franz Kafka, Max Brod and Luigi Barzini. There were also amazing dirigibles and ace pilots from around the world: the American Glenn Curtiss, the Italian Mario Calderara, and the

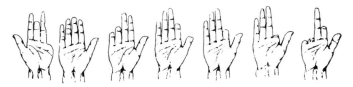

From an essay in 1909 by Kafka on the dangers of using a planing machine. Various forms of amputation that would have been insured but could have been avoided.

reigning king of the skies, Louis Blériot. In the German-language newspaper *Bohemia* Kafka published his essay 'The Aeroplanes at Brescia', full of awe and inspiration at the bravery of the pilots and the potential destructive power of the machines.

Kafka understood, given the science of his time, that modern machinery could cause traumatic accidents, which in turn could have psychological effect and even produce the grounds for physical illnesses – such as tuberculosis. Writing at the same time as the American 'muckrakers', such as Upton Sinclair (1878–1968), whose novel *The Jungle* (1906) about Chicago meat-packing inspired both George Bernard Shaw and Bertolt Brecht, Kafka's official work was directed at a much more limited audience; those who could shape policy and change the realities of the workers' lives. Here too he reflected the concerns of the 'muckrakers', so named by Theodore Roosevelt because they, like the Man with the Muckrake in *Pilgrim's Progress*, who looked down at the filth and ignored the celestial crown, exposed and attempted to correct graft and corruption in both government and business. The most famous of the Muck-rakers, in addition to Sinclair, were Lincoln Steffens and Ida Tarbell, whose major works, *The Shame of the Cities* and *History of the Standard Oil Company* respectively, appeared in 1901. They persuaded the American government to begin to think about workers' rights as well as safety in the workplace. Their parallel in Prague was Kafka's contemporary, the 'raging reporter' Hans Egon Kisch. Kafka's writing as a specialist in industrial accidents focused on the private, the limited, those disasters of the inner life, always with an eye toward the meanings given the physical body as the shell for the suffering soul. There one could have no magic restitution.

Kafka's sense of the horrors of the factory also had a private aspect. In 1911 Hermann Kafka had founded the Prague Asbestos Works Hermann & Co. to make the family's fortune. 'Hermann' was Karl Hermann, Elli Kafka's new husband, who had been lent money, Elli's dowry, at the urging of Franz to invest in the firm. Franz persuaded his bachelor uncle Alfred to invest and even put some of his own savings into the venture. Hermann Kafka 'persuaded' Franz to serve as the unpaid legal specialist and, according to his own account, Kafka became the unofficial director when his father was unable or unwilling to continue. He saw this entire undertaking as his own fault, he writes a year later to Max Brod, 'though I must have assumed this blame in a dream.'[15] His experience with the workers – unlike his experience with their claims at the insurance company – turns the 'factory into a purgatory. Why did I agree when they made me promise to work here in the afternoons? Actually, nobody twisted my arm; what forces me to go there are my father's reproaches . . . and my own guilty conscience.' Thus he writes in his diary on 28 December 1911. Suddenly Franz the good son, socialist, supporter of the worker (at least their legal claims) was the agent of the exploiters, his father and brother-in-law. Here no flight into a world of illness was possible: his father had beaten him to it with his own claims of a 'bad heart' every time something went wrong. His parents expected him to take an ever-greater role in the factory and at one point in October 1912 Kafka poses the question to Brod whether two weeks in the factory or suicide would disrupt his writing more? The factory was more than a symbol of obligation to his family; it was a real, tangible commitment to the world that demanded his unfettered attention. Unlike his work at the office, there was no one else in the 'hierarchy' on to whom Franz could pass this obligation. In 'The Judgment' much of this sense of entrapment is placed on the shoulders of the father. In reality it was a crushing weight on the shoulders of the son. (By the way, in good practical fashion Kafka opted for the two weeks straightening out things at the factory; suicide would indeed have put a greater crimp in his writing.) The factory hobbled on into the war, closing in September 1917 and finally releasing Franz from yet one more web into which he wandered, eyes wide open.

In this period of independence as he established himself as a young professional, yet simultaneously yoked to the interests of his family, Kafka also discovered an aspect of Jewish experience that had been unknown to him. While Jews in London, Frankfurt or Vienna saw Prague as part of the world of 'Eastern' Jewry, the members of the reformed congregations in Prague saw themselves as very modern and very Western. Kafka's friend Max Brod considered himself very much as a Western writer on the very fringes of the East. Kafka travelled with him to the Tyrol in 1909 and then to Paris in Autumn 1910 and again in 1911. Paris was perhaps the ideal city for the European culture maven before the first World War. What Kafka acquired on his trip in 1910 was a very bad case of furunculosis, which forced him to return home. This intense, painful and, for the time, dangerous skin disease focused his anxieties about his own body. On 20 October 1910, in Prague again, he writes to Max and Otto Brod, who were still in Paris:

A brief fainting spell deprived me of the pleasure of shouting at the doctor. I had to lie down on his sofa, and during that time – it was very odd – I felt so much like a girl that I tried with my fingers to tug down my skirt. For the rest, the doctor declared himself horrified by the appearance of my backside; the five new abscesses are no longer important since a skin eruption has appeared that is worse than all the abscesses, will take a long time to heal, and is and will be the real cause of the pain.[16]

Illness feminized his body, making him even more dependent on the care of others. But travel was not always negative. In Berlin, during a short trip in December 1910 (where he sees *Hamlet* and Arthur Schnitzler's *Anatol*), he discovered the pure pleasures of a vegetarian restaurant that fixes his rejection of all flesh. When he visited the world-renowned Berlin Aquarium, his friend Ludwig Hardt heard him mutter to the fish: 'Now I can look you in the eye with a clear conscience.'

Kafka was never Prague-bound. He made trip after trip on official business, connecting with factory owners throughout Bohemia. In May 1911 he found himself on a factory inspection trip in Warnsdorf where he sought out the health guru Moriz Schnitzer, who diagnosed him with 'poison on the spine' and suggested he do exactly what he had been doing – no meat, plenty of fresh air and (most importantly) remaining free of allopathic medicine. Doctors kill and Kafka, who dealt with them regularly in his job and his private life, suspected as much. He began to come out of his physical embarrassment: 'I have stopped being ashamed of my body in the swimming schools in Prague [and] Königssaal.'17 Yet cure was still to be sought; it was an ongoing process that enabled him to obsess about his body even in public.

If Kafka explored the West during the spring of 1910 the east had come to Prague. A Yiddish theatre troupe from Lemberg (now L'viv) appeared in the Café Savoy in May and Brod took Kafka there. Kafka was initially repelled by their 'Jargon' (the crude German label for Yiddish) and the overwhelming sentimentality of their productions. In September 1911 Kafka attended Yom Kippur, Day of Atonement, services at the Altneu (Staronová) Synagogue, the medieval hall the attic of which was said to be inhabited by the Golem, the Frankenstein's monster of Jewish Prague. He was struck by the contrast between the piety of three Eastern European Jews bowed in prayer and the ostentatiousness of the family of a well-known brothel owner. The next month, when a second theatre troupe from Galicia

Yitshak Löwy, the actor who introduced Kafka to Yiddish culture and literature.

Einladung zur Benefiz-Vorstellung

am Freitag, den 17. Januar 1913

Isaak Löwy

appeared in Prague, he was suddenly overwhelmed by the 'authenticity' of the Yiddish theater appearing at the Savoy in contrast to the 'churchlike' atmosphere of the Reformed services on Yom Kippur, by Yiddish as a 'Jewish' language and by the beauty of the actors and actresses. He was immediately infatuated by Mania Tschissik, one of the female leads, and befriended Yitshak Löwy, a Yiddish actor performing with a travelling troupe in Prague. He was especially struck by Flora Klug, who was playing men's roles. His interest was clearly obsessive since the quality of all of the plays was slightly embarrassing – if emotionally effective. Cheap theatrics can be effective theatre. For Kafka, it was an answer to the sterile sense of a Jewish ritual practice that haunted him; a practice that had become merely form for his father and without meaning for him.

The Yiddish theatre had a long history in Europe. By 1900 it was for the most part a very popular theatre intended to amuse rather than educate the masses. The plays and musicals performed were original or adaptations of 'classic' theatre, such as a Jewish version of *King Lear* with a female protagonist and a happy end. Their 'ideology' was counter to that of the Enlightenment, to educate and reform: what Kafka saw in their productions was an authenticity of Eastern Jewish experience that they themselves had fled. Typical is Kafka's response on 14 October 1911 on seeing his friend 'Löwy, whom I would admire in the dust' in a leading role:

> Yesterday evening at the Savoy. *Sulamith* by A[vraham] Goldfaden. Really an opera, but every sung play is called an operetta, even this trifle seems to me to point to an artistic endeavour that is stubborn, hasty, and passionate for the wrong reasons, that cuts across European art in a direction that is partly arbitrary.

After the performance, instead of a curtain call, Löwy was ejected from the Savoy by the head waiter because of a fight among the actors. All were acted in Yiddish, the language of Kafka's grandparents. And the setting was rather crude: baby carriages were parked in the dressing rooms; umbrellas were open backstage (and the stage was minimal) if the weather was inclement. The Prague audience came and admired the 'Rembrandt-like' appearance of the actors, according to Max Brod, who seems never to have missed a performance. The actors themselves were much less impressed with the tradition that they seemed to embody to their audience; one night Löwy shouted at Brod: 'The fanatic Eastern Jewry can impress you modern, cultivated Jews, but we are happy that we pulled ourselves out and freed ourselves from that world.' In all cases Prague, Berlin and Vienna were better than Lemberg. Brod's and Kafka's typical third-generation return to the nostalgic past merged with a more complex need.

Under Löwy's tutelage, Kafka began to study Yiddish and Jewish folklore from, of course, German texts such as Heinrich Graetz's path-breaking *History of the Jews* (1853–75), written in the Enlightenment tradition of a critique of religious excess, as well as Meyer Pines's Francophone pro-mystical *History of Yiddish Writing*. Kafka became obsessed with Jewish mythology, history and the Yiddish language, even lecturing on the Yiddish language for a Jewish public at the Jewish Town Hall in February 1912. In this talk he evokes the fear of the Prague Jews of 'the tangle of Yiddish' as a sign of the impossibility of the transformation of the Eastern Jew, and yet points out that each of his listeners knows that he or she can understand Yiddish. Is this a sign perhaps that under the nice suits and well-turned dresses they are merely Eastern Jews? No, Kafka notes, it is because Yiddish is a Germanic language, perhaps the newest one, and if his listeners would leave their inhibitions they could comprehend a new and truly Jewish culture 'intuitively'. The Eastern Jew, the 'pure' Jew, had already been discovered and transmuted by the 'dreary' Martin Buber (in Kafka's description), whose 'cultural Zionism' reshaped Eastern Jewish Hasidic tales into a form acceptable to Western Jews. (Kafka heard him lecture on 'Myth in Judaism' on 18 January 1913 and was not impressed.) Likewise, Kafka had by chance come upon the Zionist Congress in Vienna while attending a professional conference for workers' accident prevention there in September 1913. He also found Zionism no answer for his sense of a fragmented Jewish identity.

Buber's books had become bestsellers because they stressed a mystical tradition that was 'hot' at the moment in Central Europe – it was an irrationalism that permeated the contemporary reception of Nietzsche. If the central claim of nineteenth-century reform Judaism was that theirs was a rational religion, after the model of Kant's notion of Protestantism, then the Eastern Jew embodied the irrational – but for Buber and Kafka this is an acceptable irrationality because it is cast in recognizable forms. For Buber it is the fairy-tales of the German neo-Romantics; for Kafka it lies in the 'essential character of this eastern Jewish actor himself'. But just as Buber strips the magical for his notion of the irrational, Kafka represses his anxiety about the difference inherent in the image of the Eastern Jew's body. The anxiety that Kafka has about the hygiene of his new friends is clear and very Western. When Kafka took Löwy to the National Theatre in October 1911, Löwy informed him that he had gonorrhea. Kafka described his response: '[T]hen my hair touched his as I moved his head toward me, I became afraid of the possibility of lice.' The tension between attraction and infection is evident in the contact, no matter how trivial, between 'equals'. Kafka warns his listeners that at the end the fear of Yiddish is the fear of that hidden under the veneer of their own Western acculturation. Here that fear is cast in the anxiety about disease that Kafka plays with as a hypochondriac, but despairs when its reality is present.

The more Kafka revelled in his new discovery of Jewish culture the more his father dismissed it as nauseating, primitive, uncivilized. This whole thing was *Schundliteratur*, garbage literature. He had contempt for Kafka's friend Löwy, whom he compares to vermin using the very word *Ungeziefer* that Franz applies to Gregor Samsa. He saw him as little better than a wandering beggar. This became another point of conflict, even though Hermann's religious belief was at best mechanical and his knowledge of Yiddish culture certainly close to non-existent. Kafka's discovery of Yiddish as the language of itinerant players such as Yitshak Löwy comes at precisely the point in the literary history of Yiddish when its greatest authors – Sholem Aleichem (1859–1916), Isaac Loeb Peretz (1852–1915) and the young Sholem Asch (1880–1957) – were writing and being read in Prague, if only in German translation, as serious works of world literature. The same cannot be said of the roughly 20 plays that Kafka attended. But the actors were not ignorant of the stream of modern Yiddish culture. Löwy read from many of these works in his public presentations in Prague on 20 October 1911:

> Löwy read humorous sketches by Sholem Aleichem, then a
> story by Peretz, the 'Lichtverkäuferin' ('The Light Salesgirl') by
> [Morris] Rosenfeld, a poem by [Hayyim Nahman] Bialik (the
> one instance where the poet stooped from Hebrew to Yiddish,
> himself translating his original Hebrew poem into Yiddish in
> order to popularize this poem, which, by making capital out of
> the Kishinev pogrom, sought to further the Jewish cause).

A few years before, Nathan Birnbaum, a leading cultural
Zionist, had called the first conference in Czernowitz (now
Chernivtsi) to regularize the Yiddish language and make it a 'real'
language with 'real' grammatical rules. Yiddish, like Zionism,
was a burgeoning field for the modern sense of a Jewish identity
connected through literature to a deeper cultural tradition of writing at the margins. Kafka's path began with his 'discovery' of the
Eastern Jews at a point where he was still 'immensely and inex-
pressibly' indifferent to 'any form of Zionism'.[18] His connections
to this world remained close. As late as September 1917 he edited
Löwy's essay 'On the Jewish Theatre' for Martin Buber's periodical
The Jew. He sent it to Brod to forward on to Buber, which evidently
he never did. Did he feel at this point that Kafka had appropriated
Brod's own fascination for Eastern Jewry so present in his novels,
such as *The Jewess* (1911), or the numerous essays he wrote for
Buber's journal? Kafka's Jewish identity and his sense of himself
as a writer are doubly linked, for as a writer he could both be and
transcend being a Jew.

2

Writing

According to Kafka, on the night of 22 September 1912 he sat down at his desk and wrote the tale eventually called 'The Judgment'. He began writing in a cold sweat at 10 p.m. and did not stop until 6 a.m. the next morning. He had written much before, but this was the text that he saw as the beginning of his career as an author. He had published before, including two series of extracts from his much earlier unpublished 'Description of a Struggle' in the opening issue of the avant-garde poet Franz Blei's elegantly printed and very expensive bi-monthly literary journal *Hyperion* in 1908 and again in 1909. The opening chapter of a fragmentary novel jointly written with Brod under the title 'Richard and Samuel' appeared in the *Herderblätter*, edited by their friend Willy Hass in May 1912. Indeed, the avant-garde publisher Ernst Rowohlt wanted to publish a collection of his short fiction under the title of *Betrachtungen* ('Observations'). He was a productive author with a reputation that was just beginning and yet it took a moment of blinding insight on his road to Damascus to transform him into a writer in his own eyes.

'The Judgment' took Kafka's own sense of writing to a new level of creativity, as he writes in his diary next day, 23 September:

> I was hardly able to pull my legs out from under the desk, they had got so stiff from sitting. The fearful strain and joy, how the story developed before me, as if I were advancing over water.

Several times during the night I heaved my own weight on my back . . . The slight pains around my heart. The weariness that disappeared in the middle of the night . . . Many emotions carried along in the writing, joy, for example, that I shall have something beautiful for Max's [journal] *Arkadia*, thoughts about Freud, of course.

Writing is a physical act, one that projects itself into the exhausted body with a weak heart. But Kafka also knows that, as much as Freud haunted the writing of his essay, it was his relationship with a young woman that was its shadow. And we know that the 'weak heart' is his means of escaping the world that he does not want to inhabit – whether the world of work or the world of his ill father, whose demands on his son were both public (he wanted him to help with his business) and private (he doubted his ability to form lasting relationships).

The story details a struggle between Georg Bendemann and his father, regarding informing the son's friend 'in Russia' of his engagement to 'Frieda Brandenfeld, a girl from a well-to-do family'. The notion of a 'struggle' had already shaped Kafka's unpublished work, such as his 'Description of a Struggle' (1904–5). The friend is full-bearded, which does not conceal the fact that 'his skin was growing yellow as to indicate some latent disease.'[1] He is 'yellow enough to be thrown away.'[2] (The disease on the surface appears to be yellow fever; but it is a public sign of the decay of the friend. Skin colour and the beard point to fantasies about the differences of the Jews, who are assumed not to be white and to suffer from a specific skin disease, the Jewish itch (*Judenkratze*), with its telltale colour.) Unlike the diseased friend and his own father, Georg is a success in business.

'The Judgment' then proceeds to a detailed account of what turns out to be the last conversation between father and son. The father seems to be senile and weak. He cannot remember whether there really is a 'friend in St Petersburg'. Georg slowly and kindly reminds him of the friend's last visit and the stories about the 1905 Russian Revolution he told until the father exclaims: 'Of course I know your friend. He would have been a son after my own heart.'[3] The shock that accompanies this statement is matched by the father's outrage that he is marrying only because 'she lifted up her skirts like this, the nasty creature.'[4] In his impotent rage at his son, the senile father reveals that he too has been writing to the friend and has told him all. The father's tirade ends with 'An innocent child, yes, that you were, truly, but still more truly have you been a devilish human being! – And therefore I sentence you now to death by drowning.' Georg suddenly runs from the apartment, from his father, to a bridge and vaults into the river. Kafka describes Georg's last act: 'He swung himself over, like the distinguished gymnast he had once been in his youth, to his parents' pride.' Georg's last statement, masked by the sound of an approaching trolleybus, is 'Dear parents, I have always loved you, all the same.'

The family conflicts over the factory; the desire to be free from the control of his failing father; his anxiety about his father's slow physical decay; his own sporty desires for a healthy body; his new-found interest in marriage; all weave themselves into a narrative framed in the newest, modernist aesthetic of German Expressionism. Kafka knows of what he writes and he knows how to catch the eye of his desired public. Sex, fathers, Freud are in; even sport is in. Kafka's tale answers all of his readers' desires. Central to 'The Judgment', however, is the simple impossibility of any real transformation. Even with the ideal world of Georg Bendemann, with his good job and good match, he will remain what he is. His desire for improvement ends only in disaster.

The story appeared in 1913 in Max Brod's journal *Arkadia*, published by the avant-garde publisher Kurt Wolff. Brod (and Kafka) saw this annual as the 'house organ' of the 'Prague Circle'. Kafka had carefully negotiated with a number of publishing houses about bringing out his work. He spoke with Axel Juncker in Berlin and then with Ernst Rowohlt in Leipzig before settling on the new house run by Rowohlt's younger colleague Kurt Wolff. Brod served to mediate the relationship, but it is clear that Kafka knew what he was looking for in a publisher. Cautious as usual, Kafka visited Wolff in Leipzig after going to the Goethe House in Weimar in June 1912. There began (as he did almost everywhere he went) a flirtatious relationship, this time with Grete Kirchner, the teenage daughter of the house master at the Goethe House, whom he later returned to see with a box of chocolates. He was struck by her sad demeanour and the 'suppleness of her body in its loose dress'. But the serious side of the trip has to do with nailing down a publisher. Kafka is just as anxious and flirtatious about this as about the girl.

Under the arrangements that Kafka and Wolff agreed, Wolff was to be Kafka's German-language publisher until the author's death. In 1912 Wolff, having left the Rowohlt publishing house, brought out the elegantly printed *Observations*. Some of the eighteen texts are as short as one sentence and most are variations on the theme of transformation. 'Wish to Be a Red Indian' is both:

If one were only an Indian, instantly alert, and on a racing horse, leaning against the wind, kept on quivering jerkily over the quivering ground, until one shed one's spurs, for there needed no spurs, threw away the reins, for there needed no reins, and hardly saw that the land before one was smoothly shorn heath when the horse's neck and head would already be gone.[5]

Being transformed into a centaur-like creature, the rider sheds his humanness and transforms himself into the best of man and beast. This transformation is rooted in Kafka's fantasy of America rather than any acknowledgement of the classical training he received in high school. Perhaps there is a bit of the experience of his American family, for indeed Kafka, as most Central and Eastern

European Jews, had family in America. Not only had at least two of his Löwy uncles, Joseph and Alfred, travelled there on business at one time or another, his cousin Otto Kafka (1897–1939) had emigrated to the United States in 1906. There, he transformed himself into an American, learning English and working as a porter with a corset company, eventually becoming the manager of its export division. The literariness of this single sentence incorporates all of Kafka's self-awareness about the demands for and desire for physical and psychological transformation.

On 13 August 1912 Kafka had met Felice Bauer (1887–1960), a secretarial assistant, when he arrived at the home of Max Brod's father to discuss the tales with Brod. She was the cousin of Brod's brother-in-law and in Prague on business. She was the object of a flirtatious gesture (he suggested they go off to Palestine together) but by the next morning she had become his obsession. Not, one might add, the first young woman with whom Kafka was obsessed, but the one case where the obsession is tied to his self-proclaimed transformation into a writer. On 20 September he began writing a stream of about 350 of the most extraordinary letters and more than 150 postcards to this most ordinary of young women. The first was written on his office stationery two days before Kafka wrote 'The Judgment.' As the German-language Jewish Nobel Prize winner Elias Canetti notes in his reading of Kafka's letters to Felice Bauer as *Kafka's Other Trial* (1969), the most 'authentic' line in the correspondence is Kafka's claim: 'I am a mendacious creature; for me it is the only way to maintain an even keel; my boat is fragile.' Every truth is carefully crafted as a lie; and every lie is calculated to be the truth. All is as you see it; nothing is but artifice. This is not a great basis for a love story but certainly one for a fantasy of self-transformation.

According to Kafka's first impressions, Felice had a 'bony, empty face, which wore its emptiness openly. Bare throat. Blouse tossed over . . . Almost broken nose. Blonde, rather stiff, unalluring hair, strong chin.' She was a serious professional woman, the office manager of the Berlin firm Carl Lindström A. G., which produced dictating machines and record players. She represented the firm in numerous public presentations. Indeed, we have a short advertising film of her using the Parlograph, a new type of dictating machine. He writes to her on 11 November 1912 of his intense desire, but couches it in terms of physical discomfort:

> Write to me only once a week, so that your letter arrives on Sunday – for I cannot endure your daily letters, I am incapable of enduring them. For instance, I answer one of your letters, then lie in bed in apparent calm, but my heart beats through my entire body and is conscious only of you. I belong to you; there is really no other way of expressing it, and that is not strong enough. But for this very reason I don't want to know what you are wearing; it confuses me so much that I cannot deal with life; and that's why I don't want to know that you are fond of me. If I did, how could I, fool that I am, go on sitting in my office, or here at home, instead of leaping onto a train with my eyes shut and opening them only when I am with you? Oh, there is a sad, sad reason for not doing so. To make it short: My health is only just good enough for myself alone, not good enough for marriage, let alone fatherhood.

Oh! that beating, weak heart – the heart of the Kafkas – that stands between Franz and the fulfilment of his desire. Sex is for him a punishment for his desire – not its reward, as he noted in his diary entry of 14 August 1913. He imagines a celibate marriage, 'more ascetically than a bachelor, that is the only possible way for me to endure marriage. But she?' Sex with whores is fun if risky. But the horror of seeing his parents' nightclothes next to one another on their bed in the Niklasstrasse apartment he shares with them brings home what he may become: his own father.

Bachelorhood, the absence of children, is even more of a curse – the curse of the Kafkas: three of his uncles are unmarried and, even though successful, inherently unhappy with their lives. To become a father – like Hermann – or to remain a perpetual child, a bachelor; both are horrors, he writes in his diary on 24 November 1911:

> The Talmud too says: A man without a woman is no person. I had no defence this evening against such thoughts except to say to myself: 'It is now that you come, evil thoughts, now, because I am weak and have an upset stomach. You pick this time for me to think of you. You have waited for your advantage. Shame on you. Come some other time, when I am stronger. Don't exploit my condition in this way.'

It is only his body that forces him to an awareness of the horrors of the old bachelor and, of course, the fact that Valli, his middle sister, has been engaged through the good agency of a marriage broker and even Max Brod, his best friend and travelling companion, is engaged to Elsa Taussig, whom he would marry in late 1912. On New Year's Eve he writes to Felice Bauer, quoting Napoleon, 'it is terrible to die childless.'[6] That night he felt 'like a lost dog', the phrase that will echo in the closing line of *The Trial*. In the meantime Elli had given birth to her second child, which caused Franz only to have 'envy, nothing but envy . . . because I myself will never have a child.' At least not one like Franz:

> It seems so dreadful to stay a bachelor, to become an old man struggling to keep one's dignity while begging for an invitation, . . . having to admire other people's children and not even being allowed to go on saying: 'I have none myself' . . . That's how it will be, except that in reality both today and later, one will stand there with a palpable body and a real head, a real forehead, that is for smiting on with one's hand.[7]

Such is the 'Bachelor's Ill Luck' that Kafka writes in his diary of 14 November 1911. But, of course, Kafka knows that such lives are also the stuff upon which literature is crafted, as in his fragmentary, unpublished tale 'Blumfeld, an Elderly Bachelor', which his diary of 9 February 1915 describes as 'wicked, pedantic, mechanical', but reflects on the pleasures and pain of the solitary life. His mother's solution to all of this anxiety about bachelorhood was simply for Franz to get married: if he did, she commented, his health would improve, he would give up all this foolishness about writing for a living, settle down in his good job and support his family.[8] He would become normal – just like Hermann.

So the answer to being a bachelor was to be Felice – Frau Dr Kafka – or perhaps not. What did Kafka want? Felice tells Brod, who had come to Berlin and visited her, that she felt that even with the stream of letters she knew less and less about Franz. It was not until 1913 that Kafka met her three times in Berlin, visiting on one occasion the grave of Heinrich von Kleist (1777–1811), one of his most admired writers, whose life is 'very similar to mine . . . He bears me out like a friend.'[9] Kleist persuaded a young woman of fleeting acquaintance to accompany him to the shores of the Wannsee, where he killed her and then himself. A model for his engagement as well as for a life as a writer?

It was Felice whom Kafka had turned into the object of his desire as he came to imagine himself as a 'real' writer. Indeed, Kafka dedicates the publication of the story 'to Fräulein Felice B'. The line between his experienced world and his literary one was non-existent. Everything became the stuff for his writing, as he noted in his diary:

11 February [1913]. While I read the proofs of 'The Judgment', I'll write down all the relationships, which have become clear to me in the story as far as I now remember them. This is neces-sary because the story came out of me like a real birth, covered

with filth and slime, and only I have the hand that can reach to the body itself and the strength of desire to do so:

The friend is the link between father and son, he is their strongest common bond. Sitting alone at his window, Georg rummages voluptuously in this consciousness of what they have in common, believes he has his father within him, and would be at peace with everything if it were not for a fleeting, sad thoughtfulness. In the course of the story the father, with the strengthened position that the other, lesser things they share in common give him – love, devotion to the mother, loyalty to her memory, the clientele that he (the father) had been the first to acquire for the business – uses the common bond of the friend to set himself up as Georg's antagonist. Georg is left with nothing; the bride, who lives in the story only in relation to the friend, that is, to what father and son have in common, is easily driven away by the father since no marriage has yet taken place, and so she cannot penetrate the circle of blood relationship that is drawn around father and son. What they have in common is built up entirely around the father, Georg can feel it only as something foreign, something that has become independent, that he has never given enough protection, that is exposed to Russian revolutions, and only because he himself has lost everything except his awareness of the father does the judgment, which closes off his father from him completely, have so strong an effect on him.

Georg has the same number of letters as Franz. In Bendemann, 'mann' is a strengthening of 'Bende' to provide for all the as yet unforeseen possibilities in the story. But Bende has exactly the same number of letters as Kafka, and the vowel 'e' occurs in the same places as does the vowel 'a' in Kafka. Frieda has as many letters as F(elice) and the same initial, Brandenfeld has the same initial as B(auer), and in the word 'Feld' a certain connection in meaning, as well. [*Bauer* is farmer, and *Feld* is field.] Perhaps even the thought of Berlin was not without influence and the recollection of the Mark Brandenburg perhaps had some influence.

Now Kafka knew his Freud and he certainly knows his Kafka. He provides a detailed 'reading' of his own tale to reveal the mechanisms by which he (or his unconscious now made quite conscious) writes his texts. This rather reductive account seems mechanical because it is the conscious awareness of the creative process that Kafka wishes to capture in his description of the relationship of art (his tale of Georg) to life (the fictions he has spun about Felice).

Kafka's life is in his writing and this writing seems surreal, Freudian, hysterical, but is quite controlled – more Mozart than Beethoven. Max Brod saw this and printed it immediately, as Kafka knew he would the day he wrote it, in his yearbook *Arkadia*, published in Leipzig by Kurt Wolff. Wolff was to acquire a reputation as an avant-garde publisher who knew what the market wanted and delivered it to the profit of his authors and himself. Brod writes in the introduction to the first volume that he sees the yearbook as a means of fleeing the private as well as the greater politics of the world into a new aestheticism. Kafka's tale does this – transforming according to the new literary precepts the private world of his relationship to Felice and his father into what seems to be a 'purely' literary event. But Kafka knew better: he had judged the literary scene elegantly.

'The Judgment' is Kafka's first major publication and set the tone for his mode of writing – hermetic on the surface but with its meaning set in stone just beneath. But it is also the piece that he used to present himself to his audience. Kafka's first public reading of any of his work – his first appearance as a writer – was with a reading of this tale in 1912.

Following closely upon 'The Judgment' he rewrote a novel he had begun in 1911. As with 'The Judgment', it seems to pour out of him. On 29 September 1912 Max Brod noted in his diary, 'Kafka in ecstasy, writing all night. A novel set in America.' By 6 October Kafka had sat Brod down and read him 'The Judgment' and 'The Stoker', the first chapter of the novel fragment that would posthumously bear Brod's title *Amerika*. This novel mirrors the muckraking model of some of his American and German contemporaries in its ironic reversal of expectations. Written in 'ecstasy', it is of course a rewrite not only of the lost novel draft of 1911 but also of the juvenile novel of the two brothers he destroyed. The novel reflects the model of the idealistic novels of economic success, quite reversing the 'rags-to-riches' life of the classic Dickensian protagonist or those of Horatio Alger (1834–1899). Such novels are the basis for Kafka's subtle parody. From Alger's first novel, *Ragged Dick* (1867), his new genre of dime novels, known as the 'city story', heroicized the young street urchins living in poverty among large, urban centres such as New York, Boston and Philadelphia. With uncommon courage and moral fortitude, Alger's youths struggle against adversity to achieve great wealth and acclaim. This reversal is already a theme in the novels of the American muckrakers. The posthumous title, *Amerika*, is Max Brod's; today the novel is known by one of Kafka's draft titles, *The Man who Disappeared*, a title that points precisely to the anti-Alger trajectory of the protagonist.

Karl Rossmann, aged sixteen, has had a sexual misadventure with a 35-year-old housemaid who seduced him and then gave birth to his child. To spare his parents the stigma of illegitimacy, he is packed off to an uncle in America. He arrives in New York City and this frames the opening chapter with its confrontation with authority on board. Indeed the first thing that Karl Rossmann sees is the Statue of Liberty: 'the sword in her hand seemed only to just have been raised aloft, and the unchained winds blew about her form.'[10] This odd reworking of the lost early novel of America is an answer to the 'usual stuff', to Karl May's America of Saxon trappers and Indians, to Alger's ever-cheerful newspaper boys.

Here even the West has a prophetic force only as seen through the eyes of the European. Informed by his reading of Flaubert and Charles Dickens's reformist novels, such as *Oliver Twist*, it is very much in line with the interests of the muckrakers. It is an ironic reversal of the myth of America, the 'Golden Land' of the Yiddish theatre, that also became part of his image of America. It is a world in which Rossmann spirals ever downward, losing his connection with his uncle's bourgeois world of business, then becoming a n elevator operator, then a common workman. His is a tale of continuous expulsion and degradation, first from the ship with his relationship with the stoker, then with his uncle's business allies, then with the Head Cook and Head Waiter at the hotel where he is employed.

Rossmann's social and economic collapse is paralleled by precisely that transformation that would have promised success in Prague. Being a German-speaker in Prague is no more a promise of intellectual or economic success than speaking English in America. There Rossmann learns the 'native' language and thus becomes an American: 'At first the English content of his early conversations with his uncle had been confined to hello and goodbye . . . The first time Karl recited an American poem to his uncle one evening – the subject was a conflagration – it made him quite sombre with satisfaction.'[11] Unlike many of the other 'foreigners' in the novel Rossmann truly learns English well. It becomes an asset when he seeks employment at the Hotel Occidental: '"You speak German and good English, that's perfectly adequate." "But all my English I've learned in just two and a half months in America", Karl said . . . "That says everything about you", said the Head Cook. "When I think of the trouble I had learning English."'[12] Being transformed into an 'American' through speaking English is not sufficient. Rossmann remains on his downward trajectory.

Only the fragmentary account of the 'Open Air Theater of Oklahoma' seems to promise, as Kafka tells Brod, that all will be magically forgiven and that the wanderer will be returned to home and family. But when he is employed to work there he is called by the nickname 'Negro' and is introduced as 'Negro, a secondary school boy from Europe'. This moment in the novel provides one further insight into the aspects of the experienced world that he incorporates into his novel. For the question in Prague was: 'Are the Jews white?' Writing to Milena Jesenská in 1920, Kafka can comment, quite literarily, 'naturally for your father there's no difference between your husband and myself [both of them Jews]; there's no doubt about it, to the European we both have the same Negro face'[13]. But when the non-Jewish writer Jesenská herself turns, in 1938, to write about the persecution of the Jews and other minority peoples of Central Europe by the Germans, she writes about them metaphorically as 'the Negroes of Europe'. Social transformation by learning languages does not change the manner by which someone like Rossmann is seen.

Kafka had incorporated into the fragmentary final chapter a dark comic description of the 'great Theater of Oklahoma', based on his experience during July 1912 at Jungborn, Rudolph Just's naturopathic sanatorium in the Harz Mountains, where he had gone for a cure for his aching 'heart' and his 'pathological nervous condition'. Just, the son of the author of the bestselling *Return to Nature!* and purveyor of health foods, subscribed to nearly all the diet and exercise fads of the moment and he was also an advocate of nudism. Here Kafka drew the line and became known according to his own account as 'the man in the swim trunks'. Not only prudishness prevailed but a sense that he did not want to reveal his circumcised body in a place that had a New Testament in every room. His self-awareness of how the body can betray is written into the hype of the confidence men who run the 'great Theater of Oklahoma'. No promise is made here, only the inevitable final downward spiral into oblivion. Indeed Kafka's move to the 'theater' as the place to resolve all of the personal and moral dilemmas of

The sanatorium Jungborn and nudism as a means of hygiene and therapy.
Kafka wore a swimsuit.

his protagonist is a strong parodic echo of Goethe's use of that cultural institution in his *Wilhelm Meister* novels of education, except of course here the 'theater' will reveal itself not as a 'happy end' but as a confidence trick.

Kurt Wolff was so enamoured with this tale that he published the fragment of the unfinished novel as *The Stoker* in 1913; it was a success for Wolff, going into a second edition in 1916 and a third in 1917/18. What was published from the thought-experiment that was his novel was the fragment introducing the protagonist's Dickensian flight to America and his first disastrous experiences with a sword-wielding Statue of Liberty upon his arrival. Kafka's recognition as a hot new writer was immediate. In 1915 the famed playwright (and multi-millionaire) Carl Sternheim, urged by Franz Blei, turned over to Kafka the money awarded him with the Fontane Prize in recognition of the publication of *The Stoker*.

In the summer of 1913 Franz informed his parents of his intent to marry Felice and they insisted on a private detective's report

Felice Bauer,
Kafka's fiancée,
in 1914.

on the moral qualities of their future daughter-in-law. Evidently
Felice's parents did the same, having received a long letter from
Franz asking for their daughter's hand in marriage, but also point-
ing out a long list of his failings, which included his unsociability
and hypochondria. Kafka had been promoted to vice-secretary of
the Institute. Felice asked Franz to state his plans for the future.
Frozen by this demand that he see their lives together, he moans
that he 'cannot step into the future; I can crash into the future,
grind into the future, stumble into the future, this I can do; but
best of all I can lie still.'[14] This passivity is, of course, only in regard
to Felice's demand; by then Kafka had finished *The Metamorphosis*
and was reading it in a 'frenzy' to Brod. The mantra that Kafka

repeats over and over again in his letters of the time is: 'I cannot live without her, nor with her.'

Yet it is not as if Franz remained totally obsessed with Felice. In September 1913 he went to yet another sanatorium, that of a Dr von Hartungen in Riva in northern Italy, then still part of the Austro-Hungarian Empire. As with virtually of all the other such stays, he relished the fresh air and solitude, swimming and diving every day. At his communal table for meals was the young Gerti Wasner from Lübeck, small and 'Italian-looking'. She is a 'girl, a child, about eighteen years old . . . immature but remarkable.'[15] He is taken by her intense engagement with him. Their flirtation continued even after dark, with each speaking to the other from their open windows:

> I would gladly write fairy tales (why do I hate the word so?) that could please W. [Gerti Wasner] and that she might sometimes keep under the table at meals, read between courses, and blush fearfully when she noticed that the sanatorium doctor has been standing behind her for a little while now and watching her. Her excitement sometimes – or really all of the time – when she hears stories.

But most striking was Kafka's odd acknowledgement that 'For the first time I understood a Christian girl and lived almost entirely within the sphere of her influence.'[16] In his confession to Felice about the infatuation he notes that she has 'blood as alien to me as can be'.[17] Given the nature of the closed Jewish community in Prague, it is clear that most of Kafka's social interaction was with Jews. It was also clear that he had a lively sexual life with the shop-girls and prostitutes of the town, many of whom were not Jewish, though undoubtedly many of them were Eastern European Jewish women, driven by anti-Semitic violence and social upheaval to the West from the close of the nineteenth century up to World

War I. Jewish prostitutes during this period made up a visible share of the sex trade as far away as Argentina. Bertha Pappenheim, known as 'Anna O.' ('Patient Zero') in Joseph Breuer and Sigmund Freud's *Studies in Hysteria* (1895), made her career out of rescuing such Jewish prostitutes. Her view of the women she rescued was not far from that of Kafka.

Suddenly a hidden theme in the intrafamilial struggle of the Kafkas is clear: do you, like Ottla, marry for 'love' and outside of the faith (these seemed to be paired concepts, as if it were impossible to marry for love within the faith) or do you follow your parents' wishes and marry, as in Franz's case, a nice Jewish girl. The attraction for Gerti Wasner is a gesture toward the question of Franz's ability to truly make a choice and thus when she leaves the sanatorium Kafka is overwhelmed: '22 October. Too late. The sweetness of sorrow and of love. To be smiled at by her in the boat. That was most beautiful of all. Always only the desire to die and the not-yet-yielding; this alone is love.'[18] Love here is the unapproachable, the fleeting. It is associated with moments of transformation, as in the sanatorium where his life is suddenly different and seemingly better, as it is for all of us when the demands of daily life are suspended.

Kafka was taken not only by young Gerti. There was a Russian woman in the room opposite, whom he imagines he could seduce, but evidently didn't. When he returned to Prague in October 1913 he was met by the 'slim, young' Grete Bloch, a friend of Felice from Berlin. Kafka feels his engagement as a 'torture'. Later after a horrid meeting with Felice in Berlin on Saturday 8 November, at which she studiously avoided him, Kafka seemed desperate. She would only meet with him fleetingly and did not even call him when she agreed that she would. It looked as if Felice wanted to end the relationship. He returned to Prague and to the whores who would never end their reciprocity to his interest:

> I intentionally walk through the streets where there are whores. Walking past them excites me, the remote but nevertheless exis-

Grete Bloch, Felice's best friend and the lover of Franz.

tent possibility of going with one. Is that grossness? But I know no better, and doing this seems basically innocent to me and causes me almost no regret. I want only the stout, older ones, with outmoded clothes that have, however, a certain luxuriousness because of various adornments. One woman probably knows me by now. I met her this afternoon, she was not yet in her working clothes, her hair was still flat against her head, she was wearing no hat, a work blouse like a cook's, and was carrying a bundle of some sort, perhaps to the laundress. No one would have found anything exciting in her, only me. We looked at each other fleetingly. Now, in the evening, it had meanwhile grown cold, I saw her, wearing a tight-fitting, yellowish-brown coat, on the other side of the narrow street that branches off from Zeltnerstrasse, where she has her beat. I looked back at her twice, she caught the glance too, but then I really ran away from her. This uncertainty is surely the result of thinking about F.[19]

What is fascinating is how Kafka's gaze falls back on those older women whom he imagines to be like the servant-woman who took him, unhappy and resisting, to school as a child. Unlike the young and expensive whores visited by the Arconauts, here he does not have intercourse with them. They are too much like the figures of power, including Felice, who frighten him.

On New Years' Day 1914 Franz points out rather cattily all that Felice, as a professional woman, has to abandon by coming to Prague. In the meantime the Kafkas have moved to an elegant and very expensive apartment in the Oppelthaus opposite the newly renovated Jewish ghetto. He suffers in the lap of (his father's) luxury unable or unwilling to give it up. Why should he? With a mother to tend to his emotional wounds, with a father who supplies all of the little things that makes life pleasant, with a salary that he can spend on his travels to sanatoria and his whores, life should be perfect. Marriage would confound this but it would also rob him of the last shred of privacy, the privacy that he takes each evening and night to write. All of this he poured out in his letters to Felice's best friend Grete Bloch. He met Felice in Berlin for a weekend on 27 February and it became clear that Felice would not marry him because it would mean a reduction in her style of living. He suddenly looked at her and was horrified by the dental work that she had had done. True illness and deformity, even that within normal social conventions, becomes the hook on which he is able to suspend his desire. He writes to Grete Bloch that it was a ghastly meeting; 'the next time will be impalement'.[20]

Franz's mother was anxious that the engagement should continue, writing to Felice as dear daughter after the official announcement on 13 April 1914. This formally appeared in the Berlin newspapers on 21 April with acknowledgment of both sets of parents. Kafka too had

Kafka at the beach in Marielyst with an unknown friend.

written to Felice's mother as dear mother. Felice had 'taken up the cross',[21] to use Franz's odd phrase, but she expected a solid, middle-class marriage. He was now truly impaled. When Felice visited Prague to look at the suburban apartment Franz had found for them, it turns out that it was too expensive. Franz's solution is to invite Grete Bloch to share it with them: a sexual fantasy or a complete abdication of any sense of his ability to continue as a writer? Grete is suddenly aware of her implicit betrayal of her friend and refuses to function any longer as Felice's epistolary surrogate.

In July Kafka travelled to Berlin and was now confronted by Felice waving Franz's letters to Grete before his eyes. He is suddenly accused of a crime that he did not commit (but that he certainly desired to have), a romantic relationship with Felice's best friend. The scene was, according to Kafka, a trial in the Askanischer Hof hotel:

23 July 1914. The tribunal in the hotel. Trip in the cab. F[elice]'s face. She patted her hair with her hand, wiped her nose, yawned. Suddenly she gathered herself together and said very studied, hostile things she had long been saving up. The trip back with Miss Bl[och]. The room in the hotel; heat reflected from the wall across the street. Afternoon sun, in addition. Energetic waiter, almost an Eastern Jew in his manner. The courtyard noisy as a boiler factory. Bad smells. Bedbug. Crushing is a difficult decision. Chambermaid astonished: There are no bedbugs anywhere; once only did a guest find one in the corridor. At her parents'. Her mother's occasional tears. I recited my lesson. Her father understood the thing from every side. Made a special trip from Malmö to meet me, travelled all night; sat there in his shirt sleeves. They agreed that I was right, there was nothing, or not much, that could be said against me. Devilish in my innocence. Miss Bl[och]'s apparent guilt. Evening alone on a bench on Unter den Linden. Stomachache.

Was Kafka's a sin of omission (to tell Felice) or of commission? He certainly wrote to Grete in a very intimate manner but did he consummate the relationship? Grete later claimed that Kafka was the father of the child born to her in 1914 or 1915, rather than an unnamed 'friend in Munich'; the child lived until the age of seven. Franz was not the only one with an over-active and hypersexual imagination. When two such individuals meet, each finding the other a potential object of desire (what a nice young Jewish couple), it is not only the man who can have erotic fantasies.

In Kafka's account of the 'trial' everything is here: the guilt, the confrontation, the truths told, the desire revealed, the parents, the friend who loves too well, the innocent lover who is not innocent at all, the Eastern Jew, the pain of nausea – and the bedbug: one single bedbug never before seen in a room in the hotel. All self-conscious and self-aware – as if seeing oneself from a distance.

After all this Kafka's mother wrote to Felice's mother claiming that her son cannot show affection, indeed has never shown affection, even to his closest family: 'Perhaps he is not made for marriage, since his only endeavour is his writing, which is the most important thing in his life.'[22] It is this distance that makes writing possible, perhaps, but it is also certainly a means of avoiding the sort of commitments that would have transformed him into his own father.

Certainly the most important event in Kafka's world occurred in the city of Sarajevo, the capital of Bosnia, on 28 July 1914, when Franz Ferdinand, the heir to the Austrian Empire, and his wife were assassinated by Serbian nationalists. In his diary it is banally noted on 2 August 1914 that Germany had declared war on Russia and that he had gone swimming. The war furor in Prague was as intense as anywhere in the Austro-Hungarian Empire. Especially for the Jews who could 'prove' their patriotism: but to whom, the Germans or the Czechs?

> Patriotic parade. Speech by the mayor. Disappears, then reappears, and a shout in German: 'Long live our beloved monarch, hurrah!' I stand there with my malignant look. These parades are one of the most disgusting accompaniments of the war. Originated by Jewish businessmen who are German one day, Czech the next; admit this to themselves, it is true, but were never permitted to shout it out as loudly as they do now. Naturally they carry many others along with them. It was well organized. It is supposed to be repeated every evening, twice tomorrow and Sunday. (6 August 1914)

Once war actually began Franz Kafka's name was carried on the reserve rolls of the 28th Royal and Imperial Infantry Regiment. In June 1915, and again in June 1916, he was found fit for active duty (in spite of his claims of a weak heart and constitution), but was not released from his position at the Workmen's Accident Insurance

Institute for the Kingdom of Bohemia because he was considered 'indispensable' in this war work. On 11 May 1916 he discussed a long leave with the director of his Institute:

> Asked for a long leave later on, without pay of course, in the event that the war should end by fall; or, if the war goes on, for my exemption to be canceled. It was a complete lie . . . He said nothing at all about the army, as though there had been nothing in my letter about it . . . [He] made incidental remarks in the role of a lay psychiatrist, as does everyone . . . I was weak, though I knew that it was almost a life-and-death matter for me. But insisted that I wanted to join the army and that three weeks were not enough. Whereupon he put off the rest of the discussion. If he were only not so friendly and concerned![23]

Kafka's conflicting desire to serve and not to serve is complex. Could he transform himself into a soldier? One of the most powerful anti-Semitic myths of the time had Jews avoiding service because of false claims of illness: 'War stories provide many opportunities for . . . [anti-Semitism]; for instance that a sick East European Jew, the evening before his unit was marching to the front, sprayed germs of the clap into the eyes of twelve other Jews; is that possible?'[24] Jewish male bodies were seen as inherently damaged in the anti-Semitic press of the day: it was claimed that all Jews had flat feet. This disqualified them from military service.

For Kafka the image of the Jew as soldier has another, very personal level. His father had in fact been a Jewish soldier. Hermann spent three years in the Austrian army, evidently a high point in his life, quitting the service with the rank of sergeant. Indeed, the image of his father as a healthy soldier haunted even Kafka's dreams. In 1916 he dreamt of a regiment of soldiers marching by, whereupon his father comments, 'One has to see this, as long as one is able.' In 'The Judgment' the father may be ill but, in the eyes of the son, he is still 'a giant of a man'.[25] This sickly figure suddenly metamorphoses into his former self when he mocks his son because of his engagement. He accuses him of marrying only for sex: 'and mimicking her he lifted his skirt so high that one could see the scar on his thigh from his war wound'.[26] This 'war wound' marks the father's body as the soldier's body. A soldier who has served well and been wounded. Thus the 'son' who later writes to his father in the famous letter of 1919, 'You encouraged me, for instance, when I saluted and marched smartly, but I was no future soldier. . .',[27] echoes his father's desire to have a soldier as a son in order to draw his own identity into question. To be a good son and a good citizen is to be a soldier, but how can one so transform one's body?

One simple way is to demand one's autonomy as an adult. Kafka moved out of his parent's home in March 1915 at the age of 31 into a furnished room in the Lange Gasse, having first moved in with his sister Valli (her husband had been called up) as a stopgap move. His sister Elli and her two children needed his space in the family apartment in the Oppelthaus, since her husband had also been drafted at the beginning of the war. Again, it was not unusual for unmarried children to remain in their parent's dwellings until they were married – but for Kafka the link of this space to his sexual life became a literary obsession. He knew that he had 'had it too good', that he had 'grown up wholly in dependency and comfort'.[28] Place, and a quiet place at that, becomes one of the set themes in his life and work. He needs, he writes in his diary on 9 March 1914, only 'a room and a vegetarian diet, almost nothing more'. But he thinks too that he cannot marry because, in answer to Felice's imagined question: '"Are you healthy?" "No – heart, sleep, digestion."' Yet one of Felice's objections to his odd life was his vegetarianism. He needs to transform himself into a person who can marry, can have a life. He begins again to eat almost nothing but meat, which wreaks havoc with his digestion. But he does begin to write again. This masochistic gesture convinced him to again approach Felice.

Kafka's letters are seductive and clearly manipulative. They are fictions about the potential for a relationship. At the same moment he began work on what would turn out to be *The Trial*. Having experienced an unfounded but well-grounded accusation in Berlin, he is amazed to receive a letter from Grete Bloch in September. Her loyalty to her friend can now be read as a desire to see Felice and Franz apart; she coyly plays with his sense of loss and desire. In October Franz finally wrote again to Felice. He is addicted to the letters he writes her. The letter decries the perversity of writing letters – something he learned well from Grete Bloch – and declares again his love for her. Suddenly his writing spurts: he has again connected with his own fantasy. In two months he wrote 'The Penal Colony' ('In der Strafkolonie') and the central parable of *The Trial*, 'Before the Law' ('Vor dem Gesetz').

Both texts have their roots in the historical experience of the Dreyfus Affair, which was the formative political event for all European Jews of Kafka's generation. In 1894 Captain Alfred Dreyfus (1859–1935), the only Jewish officer on the French general staff, was falsely accused of having betrayed his country by selling secrets to the Germans. What resulted was a trial, banishment to Devil's Island, extraordinary public debate led by Emile Zola, a new trial, in which Dreyfus was again found guilty, and his eventual pardon in 1906. Hannah Arendt was quite right when she wrote in the late 1940s, 'not the Dreyfus case with its trials but the Dreyfus affair in its entirety offers a foregleam of the twentieth century.' It also captured the attention of every Jew from the tiny townships of Eastern Europe to the capitals of the Western, modern states.

Kafka first works through the overt question of the Dreyfus case in 'The Penal Colony' (1914). Its setting, as virtually every commentator has observed, is more than similar to Devil's Island. Indeed, even the map of Devil's Island that Dreyfus provides in his memoirs looks like the island of the fictive Penal Colony. And the primary literary source for the novel, Octave Mirabeau's *The Garden of*

Torturers (1898–9; first German translation 1902) was written under the influence of the images of the Dreyfus affair. Mirabeau himself was a Dreyfusard. Other texts, such as those by Charles Dickens on prisons and the workhouse, which have plausibly been proposed as sources, were read by Central European Jews at the turn of the century in the light of the Dreyfus trial and his punishment. It is the overriding paradigm of military life for the Jews of the age. Kafka's own family connection, via his uncle Joseph Löwy, with the 'scramble for Africa' and the founding of the Congo Society certainly brought closer a link between Jews and the horrors of the tropics. Stories about Devil's Island and the Congo were the stuff of the daily newspapers, revealing the inhumanity of the colonial world.

Yet Kafka, like Dreyfus himself in his own account, avoids any mention of the Jewishness of the prisoner. Neither the word 'Jew' nor any easily decoded reference appears in either of these texts. Kafka's prisoner, 'a stupidlooking, widemouthed creature with bewildered hair and face',[29] like Dreyfus, appears in chains, in stark contrast to the officer in his hot and stuffy, but proper, uniform. Each is Dreyfus. The latter is Dreyfus as uniformed French soldier; the former, Dreyfus in rotting rags in his cell. They turn out to be interchangeable. Indeed, the self-degradation of the officer in Kafka's tale parallels Dreyfus' degradation. He strips himself of rank and uniform and finally: 'He drew [the sword] out of the scabbard, broke it, then gathered all together, the bits of sword, the scabbard, and the belt, and flung them so violently down that they clattered in the pit.'[30] Neither the prisoner nor his guard understands the colonial language, a language different from that of the traveller/narrator; indeed, the prisoner does not speak at all. The prisoner's crime might have been to fall asleep while on guard duty, a meaningless duty, as he is to salute his officer's door every hour on the hour. He is awakened by the captain's whip and threatened: 'Throw that whip away or I'll eat you alive.'[31] The captain accuses him, which is sufficient for his condemnation ('that's the evidence'). Like Dreyfus, he is accused of a military crime, insubordination. What is central to his crime, however, is that his guilt is proven by the accusation. Kafka's sense of the order of things in war is reflected in this tale, as is his own sense of anxiety about being a Jew in a world that more and more looks at the Jews as slackers and war-profiteers. Indeed, during the course of the war the German Campaign against Anti-Semitism was to publish a statistical study showing that Jews actually served in greater numbers in proportion to their position in the population and suffered greater casualties. No one but Jews believed the book's argument, even when a volume of letters from Jewish soldiers who had died on the front was published.

The war made daily life and even cross-border travel very difficult. Kafka's job was demanding, even though his boss shared his enthusiasm for literature. Felice was distant in Berlin. In the winter, however, he met Fanny Reiss, a young woman from Lemberg. The infatuation only drew him back to his desperate sense of needing to marry and needing to see Felice. They agreed to meet on neutral territory, at a stop in Bohemia on the Prague–Berlin rail line. Coming south was not easy in the midst of war. Felice had to get a special pass to come; Franz only a railway ticket. They spent the last weekend of January 1915 there, seeing each other for the first time since the 'trial' in Berlin. Felice's flaws were again evident to him. She was a *petit bourgeoise*; he wanted to be an artist. Perhaps the final touch was when she corrected his Prague German when he ordered a meal at a restaurant. Yet when he read her 'Before the Law' she immediately grasped its meaning.

Kafka was wrestling with the fact that Felice was much more pleasant as the target of his regular letters twice monthly than in person. His social and sex life, however, seems not to have suffered. In mid-May he went to the spa at Marienbad where he had some type of flirtation (if not more) with at least six women, according to his diaries. At Felice's urging they took a vacation together in

July 1916, visiting Marienbad for ten days. While they had adjoining rooms, the door between them was kept discreetly locked. Here they again seemed to come to some type of understanding, at least Felice believed they had. Franz remained ambivalent at best. When they returned, Kafka strongly suggested that she should volunteer for Siegfried Lehmann's Jewish People's Home in Berlin, a school devoted to educating a generation of young Zionists and about which Max Brod had written. Kafka saw in her potential involvement in the school a connection to her through her Jewish identity: not as a Zionist – he was still far from seeing Zionism as the answer for the struggles of diaspora Jewry – but on a more basic level, as a person sharing a common thread of identity with himself. Felice found the suggestion odd and ignored it.

In early November 1916 Kafka appeared in Munich, again with some trouble, to read from 'The Penal Colony'. Felice came from Berlin to hear. They quarrelled again and Kafka returned home determined to find a proper place to live. He was staying in a house rented by Ottla for her assignations with her husband-to-be in the Alchimistenstrasse, but the clumsy nature of this solution was evident to both. He remained there over the winter of 1916/17 writing a series of short tales whenever Ottla did not need the space.

All the while Kafka was wrestling with his role as a son and a citizen he was carefully crafting his public reputation as the author of a series of small literary gems. Each was carefully placed (as *Observations* and 'The Judgment' had been) to provide him with the maximum audience of those he desired as his primary reader. He published in journals edited by such notable literary figures of the avant garde as Franz Blei and Ferdinand Bruckner (in his expressionistic journal *Marsyas* in 1917). Thus excerpts from the often-quoted parable 'Before the Law' appeared in the Zionist newspaper *Self-Defence* on 7 September 1915; this was part of the unpublished novel fragment *The Trial*, which he was writing in 1914 but which finally appeared posthumously.

It is *The Trial* that illustrates how 'Jewish' themes become 'modern' or 'expressionist' themes. As he had in 'The Penal Colony,' Kafka uses the tangible sense of betrayal inherent in the Dreyfus Affair in the novel. One night Dreyfus was dragged out of his bed and into an inconceivable world of betrayal, following an anonymous defamation. Or as Kafka begins his novel: 'Someone must have slandered Josef K., for one morning, without having done anything truly wrong, he was arrested.'[32] Remember the 'trial' that Kafka underwent in the hotel in Berlin. Kafka, suddenly confronted by Felice and her evidence, immediately felt himself as Captain Alfred Dreyfus, but as a Dreyfus perhaps not completely innocent of all the charges made against him. During the 'Dreyfus Affair' much was made of Dreyfus' serial seduction of young women as a sign of his corrupt character. He had not done anything 'truly wrong' but was still accused and condemned.

In the rump draft of the novel Josef K., Kafka's protagonist, both pursues his day job as an office worker in a bank, with all the politics that entails, and his social life with Fräulein Bürstner, a typist, in his boarding-house. Suddenly he must answer to these unstated charges, of which he may or may not be guilty. (Remember it was Fräulein B. to whom Kafka dedicated 'The Judgment'.)

Josef K. goes to work at his bank, where he gets a call telling him to show up for a brief inquiry into his case on Sunday. The building he discovers is a huge tenement. After threading his way through rooms and a courtyard he comes into a scene of chaos where a woman is being beaten. The court is not interested in this and K. makes his way through the crowd and leaves. Over and over the physical body is invoked in the novel as a place where danger lies and where intervention may be possible. But no intervention comes. The court, over and over, is represented not as a place of 'judgment' but of accusation, of corruption, and of infidelity. The sexual overtones at the court are paralleled by the ever-growing reticence of Fräulein Bürstner.

K.'s uncle from the country comes to visits him in his office. As in Kafka's own life, his uncle's concern with his case enables him to make the sort of connection that he appears to need. His uncle's old school chum Dr Huld, who suffers from a heart condition, has been talking to the Chief Clerk of the Court about his case. He is tended by a young nurse called Leni, who attempts to seduce K. Leni's webbed, degenerate hand fascinates him and an exultant Leni drags him onto the floor. Here again the physical anomaly points towards the moral dilemma of the characters. The stigmata of degeneration represented by the webbed hand undermine the 'natural' sexual aggressiveness of Leni as opposed to the civilized anxiety of Fräulein Bürstner.

At work K. is frightened that the Assistant Manager will take over his clients, one of whom recommends him to visit the painter Titorelli, who has had his own experiences with the court. The painter informs K. that there are various forms that his case can take: actual acquittal, apparent acquittal and protraction. Actual acquittal is impossible and never granted. Apparent acquittal is possible, but would only be followed by further arrests and trials. Protraction keeps one's case at the lowest level of the court. There are no further sudden arrests but the case must be kept active. This is the best case: protracted, unchanging ambivalence.

K. eventually fires Huld and hires a new attorney, who believes that you can tell the way a man's case will turn out by the shape of his lips. K. is going to lose his case very soon according to this rule, over which he has absolutely no control. Bodies, with their webbed hands, with their too-full or too-thin lips, always tell the truth: but no one reveals to poor K. their meaning, their hidden codes.

One of the bank's biggest clients, an Italian, arrives and K. is asked to look after him. He especially wants to see the cathedral, where he says he will meet K. When K. arrives there is no one present, apart from a priest who knows that his case is going badly, since he is clearly guilty. As they walk around the cathedral, the priest tells

K. the parable 'Before the Law': 'Before the Law stands a doorkeeper. A man from the country comes to this doorkeeper and requests admittance to the Law. But the doorkeeper says that he can't grant him admittance now.' So the man sits and waits by the door for years on end, trying to find some way to get the guard to let him in, bribing him, pleading, begging the fleas in the guard's coat to convince him to admit him. Finally, at the moment of death, he asks "'how does it happen, then, that in all these years no one but me has requested admittance." . . . "No one else could gain admittance here, because this entrance was meant solely for you. I'm going to go and shut it now."'[33]

K. and the priest discuss the parable at some length in a meaningful parody of philosophical literary criticism. Is the doorkeeper subservient to the man? Or is it the other way around? Did the man come of his own free will? Is he mad? Is the doorkeeper a mere pedant? It is not necessary to accept the world as true, only to accept it as necessary, says the priest. But, says K., then the world is based on lies. The priest reveals that he too is part of the structure of the court, which only has his best interests in mind.

A year later, on the evening before his thirty-first birthday, two men enter K.'s apartment and then, their arms entwined with his, walk him through the city. Along the way he sees Fräulein Bürstner walking in front of them, oblivious to K.'s fate. He watches her until she disappears into darkness. Finally they arrive at an abandoned quarry. They remove his coat and shirt and lay him down with a rock for a headrest. They take out a butcher's knife, apparently gesturing for him to take it and plunge it into his own chest. But he does not, instead looking across the way to a house with a light in a window. Someone is standing at the window on the top floor, and K. wonders whether it is the Judge, the High Court, which he could never reach? He holds out his hands before him, spreading his fingers. Then one of the men takes the knife and stabs him, twisting the knife twice. "'Like a dog!" he said; it seemed as if the shame was to outlive him.'[34]

Franz Kafka, like every Jew of his age, understood the fragility of his identity in terms of the Jewish Captain Alfred Dreyfus' experience of being awakened one evening and being told to come in civilian dress (for he was an army officer) to a hidden tribunal. The private nature of the novel (the appearance of Fräulein Bürstner and Leni echoing all of Kafka's anxieties about women and sex) is coupled with the public humiliation of Dreyfus. The Dreyfus Affair lasted from the first accusation in 1894 to his final pardon in 1906, but it scarred a generation of Western Jews. It was the Dreyfus *Affair*, not merely the trials of Dreyfus, that is encapsulated in the double meaning of Kafka's title *Der Prozeß*, as the totality of the experience reaches beyond the legal. In his letters, Kafka evokes Dreyfus to Max Brod as late as 1922.

Dreyfus' conviction thus defined a rupture in the Enlightenment itself for some Jews, such as the *Viennese Free Press*'s crack reporter at the trial and the public humiliation, Theodor Herzl. This is the same violation that Kafka's Josef K. experiences at the very beginning of *The Trial*: 'After all K. lived in a state governed by law, there was universal peace, all statutes were in force; who dared assault him in his own lodging?'[35] But he was not the only Jew to be so treated. In nearly every issue of the daily newspapers that Kafka read growing up in Prague there were long accounts of various and sundry 'blood libel' trials. At least fifteen cases appear between 1881 and 1900. This is the essential problem of *The Trial*, 'for someone must have slandered (*verleumdet*) Josef. K.'[36] The controversy of his trial and the authorities who eventually condemn him to being slaughtered 'like a dog' all revolve about the opening problem – who betrayed him before the very opening of the novel? What false witness denounced this petty bureaucrat living his peaceful, repetitive life? At the end of the novel, Josef K.'s guilt or innocence is unresolved, but the question of false testimony remains completely so.

Kafka's fragmentary novel about 'The Trial' is neither 'Jewish' nor 'Zionist' since it purposely has no overt reference to an external world, either private or public. But his readers would have known (had they been able to read it) exactly what the public references in the novel evoked. Dreyfus hides in the persona of K., stripped of his Jewishness in all but the physical attributes given him. His readers (and Kafka) knew how to do this sort of reading. They had all read the German adaptations by Martin Buber (1878–1965) of the Hasidic tales of Rabbi Nachmann of Bratislava (1906) and the Baal Shem Tov (1908), and knew the key to reading Kafka. (In 1917 Kafka would publish his tale 'A Dream' in one of the collected volumes compiled by the same publishing house as that in which Buber's volumes had appeared.) Buber strips the 'Eastern' magic from the texts, converting them into Western philosophical tales (with a Jewish edge); Kafka abandons even this external set of references. Buber, according to Kafka in January 1913 (in a letter to Felice), is 'dreary; there is always something missing in what he says.' He certainly does not want to be 'dreary', to write the 'usual stuff', to preach about the Jews. Yet the final scene of Josef K.'s life does evoke the binding of the unknowing Isaac, who is, unlike K., released by divine intervention.

During World War I Kafka became more and more attracted to the overtly political reading of Jewish identity offered by the Zionists. The disruption of the war brought the Hasidic 'Court' of the rabbi of Belz to Prague and Kafka visited him together with his newly Orthodox friend Jiří Langer. He was both attracted and repelled by the exoticism of this world, which embodied for him both spirituality and dirt. The balance to this Yiddish-speaking world Kafka found in Zionism and its emphasis on Hebrew as the spoken language of the Jews. Kafka began to study Hebrew as a means of 'strengthening his Jewish consciousness', paraphrasing the Zionist call of the Basel programme. When his friend Miriam Singer, with whom he studied Hebrew during the war, returned to Prague from Palestine in 1919 he gave her a copy of his *Country*

Doctor, commenting that she was much too healthy to understand him. One of the central claims of political Zionism was the need to reform the diseased Jewish body into a healthy modern one capable of being a farmer (and a soldier). This transformation was part of the ideology of modern Hebrew that Kafka could not share. Yet Kafka continued to study Hebrew, reading and writing an elementary version of the language. As late at 1923 he studied with Puah Ben-Tovim who had come from Palestine to study in Prague, sent by Kafka's friend Hugo Bergmann, who was organizing the library at the nascent Hebrew University. She was bilingual in German and Hebrew and was heralded as the 'first native Hebrew-speaking bird from the old-new land'. Kafka was impressed by her and studied Hebrew; he was equally impressed by her lineage, as her father Zalman Ben-Tovim was a leading Hebrew writer. Is Hebrew the once and future language for the Jewish writer? he thought, echoing a major debate of the time. In 1916 Max Brod argued against Martin Buber that 'Jewish' poetry could be written in languages other than Hebrew and that there were 'Jewish writers of the German tongue'. Kafka himself noted that Jewish writing in German is a 'literature impossible in all respects'. Jewish writing in German becomes 'a Gypsy literature which had stolen the German child out its cradle and in great haste put it through some kind of training, for someone has to dance on the tightrope'.[37]

Brod held that Kafka was the greatest living 'Jewish writer of the German tongue'. Buber agreed and invited him to submit tales to his radical periodical *The Jew* in 1917. Kafka responded with his two 'animal tales', 'Jackals and Arabs' and his extraordinary 'A Report for an Academy', the tale of the monkey Rotpeter, who learns to become a man to his own sorrow. Both tales reflect quite directly on the demon that Kafka sees among the Reform Jews of Western Europe – the need to but also the impossibility of transforming themselves into something, anything else. But his publishing strategy is also clear – the avant-garde and the Jewish, the Jewish and the avant-garde are his two audiences; they overlap and provide quite different readings of his texts. He plays with his audiences, knowing full well their expectations and his ability to answer and manipulate them.

No text of Kafka's reveals this double set of readers more clearly than what is certainly his best-known short story 'The Metamorphosis' ('Die Verwandlung'). It had been conceived during the first moment of his epistolary passion for Felice Bauer; he mentions a 'little story' to her as early as November 1912.[38] Kafka read with great pleasure the opening of the tale to Brod and Oskar Baum on 24 November. He wrote to Felice about his reading, wishing that she too had been there, but also complaining that his need to turn up at the office had damaged the flow of the tale. If only he had the ability to be a writer full-time like his friend Franz Werfel, who was now working for Rowohlt in Leipzig and writing his poetry! For it is the solitary act of writing that gives him the most pleasure. His mother had sensed the other side of her son when she suggested he marry: she attributed his physical and emotional fragility to that other solitary act, masturbation. If Felice satisfied the one desire, she destroyed the other: 'If I were with you I'm afraid I should never leave you alone – and yet my craving to be alone is continuous', he writes to her.[39]

While 'The Metamorphosis' has become the standard translation of the title into English (and French), the resonance in English to Ovid's *Metamorphoses* masks the actual meaning of the title, which is much closer to 'Transformation' in a biological sense. What Kafka presents in the tale is the complete transformation of a young man into that which he could never have imagined. Published in 1915 by Kurt Wolff, the title page shows a man turning away in horror from a partially opened door. Nothing but darkness can be seen within. We know what has happened: 'As Gregor Samsa awoke one morning from uneasy dreams he found himself transformed in his bed into a gigantic insect.'[40] The transformation into a bug had been a

The cover of Kafka's 'The Metamorphosis'. Kafka refused to allow the illustrator Ottmar Starke to create an image of Gregor Samsa.

FRANZ KAFKA

DIE VERWANDLUNG

DER JÜNGSTE TAG • 22/23
KURT WOLFF VERLAG · LEIPZIG
1 9 1 6

theme in Kafka's sense of his own body. He had dreamt of himself as a huge bug, saw bugs in perfectly clean hotel rooms, and now would capture the anxiety of transformation from human into bug. He had sketched such a reverse transition from ape into human in one of his tales for Buber, mirroring the ironic path that European Jews had taken since the Enlightenment. (Were they now truly 'human' or merely a simulacrum of what humans imagined themselves to be?) Now the question is posed, as with Josef K.'s sudden transformation into an accused, was the transformation of human into an insect truly a change of status or had he always been so 'in reality'?

Gregor Samsa is a conscientious travelling salesman who seems more concerned with being late for his morning train than with the transformation he has undergone. Gregor lies in bed contemplating a picture of a 'lady, with a fur cap on and a fur stole, sitting upright and holding out to the spectator a huge fur muff into which the whole of her forearm had vanished.'[41] This image, with its clear reference to *Venus in Furs* (1869), the classic tale of male masochism by Leopold Sacher-Masoch (1836–1895), becomes a theme in charting the decline of the protagonist into his insect state. He still lives with his parents. Grete, his seventeen-year-old younger sister, is appalled at his tardiness, as is the chief clerk who comes to enquire about him. The chief clerk assumes that he is malingering and threatens to call the insurance doctor. He could not really be ill. All are horrified when he manages to open the locked door with his mandibles and appears. His mother's response is that he is ill and that Grete must go for the doctor. But no medicine can cure Gregor's transformation. Still Gregor relates to picture and door and the inhabitants of the apartment as if he were human, that is, 'not ill'. This charts the beginning of his transformation into the 'essence of an insect'.

When his sister comes to give him food, Gregor realizes that the fresh milk and bread is unpalatable. He revels when she gives him garbage and water. It is Grete who understands this and quickly becomes his sole connection with the outside world. His parents wish to ignore him as a bad dream. Yet now that he is no longer earning the money to support the family, his father must go to work. This fact transforms him from a weak and dependent figure to the breadwinner. Gregor has abdicated his role in the family and the 'natural order' is now restored.

As time passes Gregor becomes more and more bug-like. He spends his days crawling over the walls. To facilitate this Grete removes more and more of the furniture from the room. When she goes to remove the picture of the lady in fur Gregor responds: 'he was struck by the picture of the lady muffled in so much fur and quickly crawled up to it and pressed himself to the glass, which was a good surface to hold on to and comfort his hot belly.'[42] If at the very beginning of his transformation he sees the image and understands the erotic impulse that made him clip it from a magazine and frame it, at this point he relates to it as a cool spot on the wall that comforts his insect body. Grete suddenly sees him – he has hidden behind the furniture up to this point – and is horrified, throwing a bottle of corrosive medicine at him. Again no medicine can help; it only infuriates him and he leaves the room. His father, now 'dressed in a smart blue uniform with gold buttons', throws apples at him to drive him back into his own, now empty chamber. It is the father who is clearly in charge. Gregor has become a freakish burden.

The family is forced to take in boarders to make ends meet. They also hire an old charwoman to take over Grete's obligations in caring for Gregor. After an incident in which Gregor appears to listen to his sister play the violin for the boarders, the last grasp of his humanity, Grete takes charge and demands that they must rid themselves of this creature, who is not her brother but a giant insect: 'things can't go on like this . . . I won't utter my brother's name in the presence of this creature, and so all I say is: we must get rid of it.'[43] The transformation is complete – at least in the eyes of the beholders, for they argue that, if this were truly Gregor, he would have realized that humans could not live with such a creature, and would go away. Gregor returns to his room, ruminating about his family 'with tenderness and love', until he dies at three in the morning.

Next morning the cleaning lady finds him and reports to the family: 'Just look at this, it's dead; it's lying here dead and done for!'[44] The family sees the corpse and crosses themselves as Mr Samsa says: 'Now thanks be to God.' (Clearly, the Kafka family have been successfully transformed into Christians by this point.) The boarders are ordered from the apartment. The cleaning lady gets rid of the corpse: the father decides that she too will be dismissed. The family takes the tram out to the country to discuss their future. They will leave the old apartment and improve their lot. As they return the parents notice that Grete too has been transformed during Gregor's period as an insect. She has become a 'pretty girl with a good figure' and unconsciously knows that soon it will be time to find a good husband for her. 'And it was like a confirmation of their new dreams and excellent intentions that at the end of their journey their daughter sprang to her feet first and stretched her young body.'[45]

The tale of the man become physically a bug, of a young girl's transmutation into a woman, of a family able to deal with economic difficulty and their son's voyage through the realm of being a bug towards a death beyond the help of modern medicine is well suited to Kafka's model of multiple, hidden readings. Remember Kafka's oddly mechanical reading of the names from 'The Judgment' – Samsa is an easy equivalent for 'Kafka'. But what does this transformation mean? It is a portmanteau transformation. It is as much the decay of the Jews of the West into non-functional members of their own community as much as it is the transformation of the son in a dysfunctional family, with an ill (or hypochondriacal) father, a passive mother, and a sister entering into her own sexual awareness. All of this is present and yet none of this is dominant. It has always been possible to read the tale in many ways, filling in the cultural references based on those approved by the interpretative community in which one found oneself. No deep knowledge of Freudian psychology was necessary for Kafka to write in this encrypted manner. You only had to know enough psychological theory from the daily papers or contemporary literature, for example the writings of Freud's friend Arthur Schnitzler (1862–1931), to appreciate and believe you understood the family dynamics as mirroring the cultural politics of the Jews of Central Europe. Kafka passes this through Freud's Oedipus with a bit of sibling incest and Jewish self-loathing thrown in for fun.

The notion of a permanent transformation that is in no way

your doing, but blocks your understanding of your own life and world, is simultaneously a comment on the modern, technological age of mass killing that was World War I as well as the status of the Jew in Kafka's Europe. You are not in control of your life exactly as it is being changed. It is the theme of *The Trial*. But it came to have even further meaning for Kafka's own life. His hypochondria was his salvation. It rescued him from jobs he did not like and relationships with those, especially women, whom he feared. As early as 14 June 1914 he wrote to Felice Bauer: 'This state of health is also deceptive, it deceives even me; at any moment I am liable to be assailed by the most detailed and precise imaginings and invariably on the most inconvenient occasions. Undoubtedly an enormous hypochondria, which however has struck so many and such deep roots within me that I stand or fall with it.'[46]

With his move into rooms in the Schönborn Palace in 1917, which

The Schönborn Palace, Marktgasse 15, where Kafka lived from March 1917 and where he first manifested the symptoms of tuberculosis in August of that year.

The engagement photograph: Kafka and Felice in Budapest in July 1917.

he imagined he would occupy as a married man, in July Kafka again asked Felice to marry him, an engagement that lasted until the end of that year. The Schönborn Palace had been cut up into apartments (and is today the US Embassy). Since leaving the family home in 1914 he had lived in a series of apartments and rooms all over Prague.

Finally he found a place that seemed appropriate to his sense of self and which would potentially be acceptable to his past and present fiancée, Felice Bauer: 'I went into a housing bureau, where, almost immediately, I was told of a flat in one of the most beautiful palaces . . . It was like the fulfilment of a dream. I went there. Rooms high and beautiful, red and gold, almost like in Versailles. Four windows overlooking a completely hidden quiet courtyard, one window onto the garden. What a garden! When you enter the gate of the palace you can hardly believe what you see.' No kitchen, no bathroom – but isolation in decaying grandeur. It was there that Kafka finally became ill. Leaving the damp and mouldering rooms after the onset of his illness, on 2 September he wrote to Ottla, saying that he has closed his 'cold, stale, ill-smelling' apartment: 'And so I leave. Closing the windows in the Palace for the last time, locking the door. How similar that must be to dying.' And dying he was. Kafka's illness turned out to be none of the 'family' illnesses – neither his father's weak heart nor his mother's family 'madness.' He returned to the family apartment, moving into Ottla's old room next to the toilet, illness branding him again a failure as a son and his parents' 'kaddish', the one who must recite the memorial prayers after their deaths. He 'could not pass on the family name . . . consumptive and, as the father quite properly sees it, having gotten sick through his own fault, for he was no longer released from the nursery for the first time when, with his total incapacity for independence, he sought out that unhealthy room at the Schönborn Palace.'47

In early August 1917 Kafka had suffered a tubercular haemorrhage in the early morning hours, awaking with a mouthful of blood. He kept this secret to himself until the very end of the month when he revealed it to Ottla. He first writes about the outbreak of his illness to Felice on 9 September 1917:

I had a haemorrhage of the lung. Fairly severe; for 10 minutes or more it gushed out of my throat; I thought it would never stop.

The next day I went to see a doctor, who on this and several subsequent occasions examined and X-rayed me; and then, at Max's insistence, I went to see a specialist. Without going into all the medical details, the outcome is that I have tuberculosis in both lungs. That I should suddenly develop some disease did not surprise me; nor did the sight of blood; for years my insomnia and headaches have invited a serious illness, and ultimately my maltreated blood had to burst forth; but that it should be of all things tuberculosis, that at the age of 34 I should be struck down overnight, with not a single predecessor anywhere in the family – this does surprise me. Well, I have to accept it; actually, my headaches seem to have been washed away with the flow of blood.[48]

It becomes a metaphor for his life (and this is Kafka writing, not Susan Sontag), as he wrote in his diary during September 1917:

You have the chance, as far as it is at all possible, to make a new beginning. Don't throw it away. If you insist on digging deep into yourself, you won't be able to avoid the muck that will well up. But don't wallow in it. If the infection in your lungs is only a symbol, as you say, a symbol of the infection whose inflammation is called F[elice], and whose depth is its deep justification; if this is so then the medical advice (light, air, sun, rest) is also a symbol. Lay hold of this symbol.[49]

Kafka's tuberculosis was a relief for him. Here was a disease that he could claim as his own, not as a curse from his parents. He went to his family physician, Dr Mühlstein, who diagnosed it as a catarrh. When asked whether it could be tuberculosis, he shrugged his shoulders, noting that everyone has tuberculosis and if it were a shot of tuberculin would cure it. (That was the 'magic bullet' developed by the discoverer of the tuberculosis bacillus, Robert Koch. Sadly it was not very effective.) Actually his doctor's view was the common wisdom of the day. Emil Cohnheim, one of the greatest experts on the disease, noted that everyone had tuberculosis, but only a few came down with symptoms. Since one could test for exposure to the disease, it was clear that everyone did test positive – why then did only some people develop symptoms? Or rather, why did some people not develop symptoms? Indeed, common knowledge, which he was well aware of from his professional work, claimed that Jews were resistant to tuberculosis, that it was a disease of the *goyim*, the non-Jews. But during the cold, wet, hungry months of 1916 the incidents of tuberculosis soared for everyone, especially the Jews. Indeed, Jewish mortality from tuberculosis doubled in Berlin between 1913 and 1917, an increase much greater than among the general population. But the Jews in the East also saw spectacular increases up to 1917. Indeed that year seems to have been the pinnacle for increases among all groups, but especially among the Jews. In Vilnius there was a 90 per cent increase in Jews dying from tuberculosis between 1916 (208 deaths) and 1917 (496 deaths). In Bialystok, the rate among Jews went from 46.6 deaths from tuberculosis for every 10,000 Jews in 1916 to 72.8 in 1917. In Vienna, the mortality from tuberculosis among Jews in 1919 was 186 per cent higher than in 1913/14. The reasons are evident: the extraordinary severity of the winter and the poorer food available in the cities, especially in the East. Kafka in his windy and clammy castle was certainly more at risk than most. The disease also progressed more quickly because of the lower resistance caused by poor nutrition. When, on 4 September, he went at Max Brod's insistence to the university clinic directed by Professor Friedl Pick, he found Mühlstein's diagnosis confirmed. Pick suggested an extended stay in a sanatorium, the standard treatment of the day, and Kafka asked for leave from his job. He tells his parents, however, that he needs the leave because of his 'nerves'.

On 9 September he had written to Felice about his illness. From that moment (if not before) it was clear to Franz that his somatic

Kafka's passport photograph in 1920.

illness was an answer to his inner conflicts. When Felice came to
Prague from Berlin in mid-September Kafka's guilt was overwhelming: 'she is an innocent person condemned to extreme torture; I am
guilty of the wrong for which she is being tortured, and am in
addition the torturer'. Now Felice is Dreyfus. When she returned to
Berlin, Kafka wrote and broke off the engagement for a second time.
'The blood issues not from the lung', Kafka writes, 'but from a deci-
sive stab delivered by one of the combatants.'[50] Suddenly she was

gone from his life and Kafka wept, sitting in Brod's office bemoaning his treatment of her. Kafka stayed with Ottla in the country until April 1918. When Felice finally did marry in 1919, it was not to Franz Kafka but to a Berlin businessman, but she never forgot him, even taking his extensive letters with her when she escaped Europe and the Nazis with her family for America – here the real America, not Kafka's fantasy.

Franz Kafka, so long afraid that he would become ill, was now truly ill and with a disease that seemed to have both cultural significance (even if you did not get to the Magic Mountain of the Swiss clinics) and personal meaning. How would he cope with actually being ill?

Some of Kafka's own
sketches from his
diaries.

3

A Life ill

Closing the rooms in the Schönborn Palace and moving back to his parents' apartment meant acknowledging his illness. He fled Prague and, as we have seen, his obligations to Felice. Between late 1917 and April 1918 he lived in the farmhouse in Zürau in north-western Bohemia that his sister Ottla occupied with the non-Jewish Jakob David (1891–1962). (Their two daughters Vera and Helene were born only in the early 1920s. After the outbreak of his illness Franz took a role as a surrogate child in their relationship.) There Kafka began to read Kierkegaard and write a series of aphorisms about 'the last things'. He ruminates in a letter to Brod in mid-November that perhaps Flaubert was right and that there are people who are *dans le vrai*. Like the 36 righteous Jews hidden in each generation, perhaps there are people (and here he means himself) whose lives are truer in their suffering. He had been left in this mood by Felice's final visit. Yet it was Ottla who managed to stabilize her brother. Franz had a close relationship with his strong-minded sister, who would regularly confront their father until he grasped at his chest and won their arguments by calling on his bad heart. She had been involved with his business, serving as his bookkeeper. It was Hermann who had got Franz involved with a failed asbestos factory, which was a disaster for everyone. His arguments with Franz rarely ended with his son winning, as he always had the trump card: You danced me into this, he would say, and then you left me 'in the lurch'.[1] At the beginning of May 1918, Kafka returned to work at the Institute. For months a manuscript of short tales had been lying on the desk of Kurt Wolff, who speaks to Erich Reiss and Ernst Rowohlt about it. Suddenly Wolff has it in print.

Kafka's illness begins to haunt his writing in an ever more overt manner. Many of the works he wrote after he became ill refer in complex ways to disease and death, but this had also been his topic prior to his haemorrhage. In 1919 he published the collection with the title story 'A Country Doctor', but this was most probably written during the war winter of 1916/17 that preceded the diagnosis of tuberculosis (and which also saw a spectacular increase of the disease in Prague). Dedicated to his father (with no irony), he hoped that it would bring, if not a reconciliation between them, at least a sense that he was trying for one: 'I will have done something, not perhaps settled in Palestine, but at least travelled there with my finger on the map.' The title story first appeared in a literary almanac, *Die neue Dichtung* (The New Writing), in 1918. As with one central aspect of 'The Metamorphosis', it is an account of a failed cure and the meaninglessness of modern, Western medicine. To begin at the beginning: One evening the country doctor, actually the regional health officer, is called out on an emergency. At a loss as to how he is to get to his patient, a groom suddenly appears. Magic horses also appear out of his abandoned pigsty to pull his carriage. As he is about to depart the groom suddenly turns on his maid, Rosa: 'Yet hardly was she [Rosa] beside him when the groom clipped hold of her and pushed his face against hers. She screamed and fled back to me; on her cheek stood out in red the marks of two rows of teeth.'[2] The mark on the cheek is the first sign of something being wrong with the representations of the characters' bodies in the story: a sign of something out of joint. It is a visible sign of the destruction presented by the introduction of illness into the tale, for without the call to the patient, who is ill, none of the magic would have been needed. We, through the eyes of the country doctor, see the marks on Rosa's cheek and we know their cause – the bite of the groom. But this is, of course, only the proximate cause, the sign now written on the body. The ultimate cause seems to be the illness of the patient. It is diagnosis that is identifying causation that fails at this point.

While the doctor threatens the groom with a beating, he is also made internally aware (as we are) that the groom has appeared to help him to reach the patient and therefore cannot be punished, since the patient must (according to the Hippocratic oath) take precedence. We read this in his thoughts as revealed by the narrator. So he is forced to abandon Rosa to the further attacks of the groom while the horses carry him to his patient. Sexuality, destruction and illness are all linked in the wound on the maid's cheek. This image is also indicative of the problem of Western medicine representing the rationality of the Enlightenment in trying to understand its multiple roles in a complex society.

When the doctor magically reaches his patient, he provides us with an account of the visual and tactile nature of the patient's appearance: 'Gaunt, without any fever, not cold, not warm, with vacant eyes, without a shirt, the youngster heaved himself up from under the feather bedding.'[3] Having given this physical examination, the doctor dismisses the patient as a malingerer until he is forced by his family to examine him further. At that point he discovers the tumour: 'In his right side, near the hip, was an open wound as big as the palm of my hand. Rose-red, in many variations of shade, dark in the hollows, lighter at the edges, softly granulated, with irregular clots of blood, open as a surface mine to the daylight.'[4] This is the vision of a cancerous lesion as well as a syphilitic one, at least in its literary provenance. It is the mythic Grail king's wound to be healed by the errant knight Parsifal (with Richard Wagner's music being quietly hummed in the background). It is the wound in the groin that marks the appearance of illness, sexuality and destruction. And being rose-coloured it is linked to the maid's cheek visually and literally. The visual link is evoked in the colour as well as the visualization of the word. The doctor now feels that he cannot act at all. The case is hopeless. When the patient asked to be left alone to die, the doctor had suddenly been brought to think about that other hopeless case, Rose, whom he had abandoned some ten miles away.

He continues to examine the lesion. In it he finds further proof of the impossibility of a cure. The wound was full of 'worms, as thick and as long as my little finger'.[5] The maggots in the wound are read by the doctor as a sign of putrefaction, of the inevitability of his patient's death from the now open tumour. He of course was wrong in this reading. He was brought by the magic horses and through the actions of the magic groom not to evoke the powers of Western medicine but to bring his shamanic authority as a healer to the bedside. The medical world into which he has entered is the world of folk medicine. His modern, Western, enlightened skills may well be useless, perhaps more owing to his own ambivalence about them than because of any innate problem with the medicine itself. It is the doctor, not the medicine, that is at fault. The model of medicine that he brings into the country house forces him to misconstrue the meaning of the larvae. Maggot therapy is an old folk (and present-day clinical) remedy for precisely cleaning ulceration. It had been recognized as a successful means for the debridement of wounds in folk medicine for at least four hundred years before Kafka wrote his tale. By the 1920s the use of maggot therapy had even become part of clinical practice. The line between folk medicine and clinical practice is always slippery but, from the perspective of the clinician, needs always to be distinguished from 'quackery'. The doctor's misdiagnosis of this folk remedy shows him that his only role is to become part of the magical treatment of the child. He is lifted up by the family and laid in the patient's bed magically to warm and cure the child's lesion. When he is laid on the bed, the boy says to him: "'I have little confidence in you. Why, you were only blown in here, you didn't come on your own feet.'"[6]

The Jewish foot that made it impossible in the anti-Semites's imagination for the Jew to become a soldier was also the malformed foot of the limping, goat-footed devil and Kafka's limp with which he frightens Elli's daughter: 'I frightened Gerti [Kafka's young niece] by limping; the horror of the club foot.'[7] The damaged foot suddenly reappears as the definition of the doctor so dependent on Western medicine that he is impotent.

Kafka's country doctor uncle Siegfried Löwy may have served as a model for the protagonist, but his vocabulary of images that deal with illness and bodily decay is taken from his own world. How could it be otherwise? What is removed is the Jewish aspect in Kafka's bodies. Everything else is left. Kafka universalizes the literary discourse of his texts by deracializing it, incidentally as does Tomáš Masaryk in the founding of the Czechoslovak Republic. There, following the Treaty of Versailles, the Jews formed a 'national' rather than a 'religious' minority. As such they were eligible for political representation but they were also no longer analogous to Catholics, Protestants and Free Church members. They were again transformed. While some of his contemporaries, such as Richard Beer-Hoffmann and Arnold Zweig, were moving in precisely the opposite direction, by thematicizing Jewishness, Kafka was removing the overt references to the Jewish body from his work. What are left, of course, are the images without their racial references. And yet they would have been present in any contemporary reading of the text. The association between sexuality and syphilis, the association of specific predisposition to specific forms of tumours, were part of the legend of the Jewish body at the turn of the century. One further association that is quite powerful is the image of the Jews as physicians that haunts the anti-Semitic literature of the time, as well as the work of Jewish physicians such as Arthur Schnitzler.

In the tale of Kafka's country doctor, the Jewish references are totally missing. Yet their traces, following Kafka's reading of Freud's theory of the dream, are also present. Let us imagine that Kafka consciously adapts a Freudian model rather than thinking that this is all a process of unconscious forces. Kafka knows clearly that his texts are to be avant-garde, that the model he strives for is a reading of his texts, not as a Jewish writer with all of the anti-Semitic taints ascribed to that category, but rather as a 'modern' writer. The imagery he draws on are the images from which he wishes to distance himself. They are present in an overt language: the tumour of the cheek, the lesion in the groin marks the presence of disease. The unsure-footedness ascribed to the physician and his inability to read the folk medicine he sees (and becomes part of) mirrors the sense of being caught between rival claims. On the one hand was the claim of the Enlightenment on the Jew as a rational being, espousing a 'scientific' religion that prefigured much of modern medicine. On the other hand was the desire of Central European Jews at the turn of the century to be different, to express their Jewishness in their own manner, even to revelling in the irrational and the magical. Leopold Sacher-Masoch, the author of Gregor Samsa's favourite work of art, had presented this dichotomy in 1892 in 'Two Doctors', his key text on the nature of Austrian Jews, contrasting and reconciling the two types. For him, a late Enlightenment (and non-Jewish) writer, 'modern' medicine is recognized by the practitioner of folk medicine as preferable and 'wins' over the competition. Jews of Kafka's generation are no longer so secure in this assumption. Perhaps the lost truths of ancient belief and practice were in their particularism more valuable for the modern Jew than acculturation? In 'A Country Doctor' Kafka too uses the physician as the model for the conflict between rationality and irrationality, but it is quite clear as to which force will win. The forces of the irrational triumph because the doctor cannot understand what he sees through the lens of his rationality. This too was the dilemma seen by Jews of Kafka's generation. It echoes in their writing and their desire for a place for the irrational, for the messianic, for the transcendental in the world.

With the end of the war all was being rethought in Prague. On the public level Kafka returned to his job, soon to be a Czech civil servant. His real illness meant that he could now ask to be relieved of work, much like Gregor Samsa, and he applied to get his pension. He entered his first request on 6 September 1917; this was granted only in July 1922 after numerous extended leaves owing to his ever-worsening health. During the autumn of 1918 he survived the first (and weaker) round of the 'Spanish Flu', which was a pandemic killing millions. At the same time the conflicts in his private life exacerbated. At the end of 1918 he was taken by his mother to the Pension Stüdl, a rest home for those suffering from tuberculosis, in Schelesen (now Íelizy), a small town near the Elbe River in the hill country northwest of Prague. There he met the thirty-year-old Julie Wohryzek, the daughter of a shoemaker and synagogue custodian (*shammes*) from Prague. To Franz she appeared to belong to 'the race of shop-girls', not too bright nor too attractive but available. 'Not Jewish and yet not not-Jewish, not German and yet not not-German, crazy about the movies, about operettas and comedies, wears face powder and veils, in general very ignorant, more cheerful than sad.'[8] And in her case also ill. By the spring of 1919 they were engaged to be married that November. His father strenuously objected because of her low social status. According to Franz his father shouted:

> She probably put on a fancy blouse, something these Prague Jewesses are good at, and right away, of course, you decided to marry her. And that as fast as possible, in a week, tomorrow, today. I can't understand you: after all, you're a grown man, you live in the city, and you don't know what to do but marry the first girl who comes along. Isn't there anything else you can do? If you're frightened, I'll go with you.

This account is reported in the unsent 'Letter to a Father', written in 1919 when the conflict with Hermann had reached its peak,

Julie Wohryzek in a photograph from the period of the First World War.

at least in Franz's eye. In November 1919 he was back in Schelesen and penned the letter to his father, more than 60 (printed) pages in length, that summarizes his life and loss – and attributes all of his daily horrors to Hermann, now aged and exhausted. His gesture of wanting to dedicate *A Country Doctor* to him has not dispelled the ghosts. The engagement to Julie peters out. His suggestion that they move together to Munich is unworkable. Kafka wants to retain some type of connection with her but sees that marriage is not a reasonable culmination of their relationship – because of *her* illness. Kafka postponed the wedding in November 1919 but ended the engagement officially only in July 1920. Again the father seems to win – but Kafka had carefully created a father who had to win and thus Franz himself could avoid yet another entangling relationship. And this is for him typically Jewish, even to the use of psychoanalysis to explain it, as was mentioned at the beginning of this book. Kafka's life seems also much like that of the Prague Jews he described in June 1921: 'Psychoanalysis lays stress on the father-complex, and many find the concept intellectually fruitful. In this case I prefer another version, where the issue revolves not around the innocent father but around the father's Jewishness.' Such a father is a good thing, maybe even a necessary thing to have – if you are Franz Kafka and in November 1920 the worst anti-Semitic riots in a decade are taking place on the streets of Prague. Kafka writes to Milena Jesenská: 'Isn't it an obvious course to leave a place where one is so hated? . . . The heroism which consists of staying on in spite of it all is that of cockroaches which also can't be exterminated from the bathroom.'[9] Here he means Prague, not his family – but they are often interchangeable. Again he feels himself as Dreyfus existing with the 'loathsome disgrace of living all the time under protection'.

In 1919 Kafka had received a letter from the 25-year-old Milena Jesenská-Pollak (1896–1944), Christian and Czech, who wanted to translate 'The Stoker' into Czech. Married (against her father's wishes) to the German-Jewish Ernst Pollak, she was part of the serious avant-garde art scene in Vienna. She claimed that she had met Kafka in Prague the previous year, though he had only a vague memory of the meeting. Kafka had an intense, highly charged exchange with her while recuperating in a sanatorium in the Tyrol. In the course of their letters he finally abandoned the notion of marrying Julie. He finally travelled to Vienna to meet her between 29 June and 4 July 1920. Their walk in the woods was, at least according to his letters, the moment when they consummated their relationship. Upon his return to Prague he again slept with Julie. He told her that he had fallen in love with Milena. She was crushed and wished to write to his new love. When Milena responded it was clear that Julie's relationship was over and she vanished from Kafka's life, as so many young women had done in the past.

Kafka's letters to Milena, as with all of his correspondences with young women, are full of ardour and timidity. He writes to her in German, but insists that she answer him in Czech:

> No, Milená, I beg you once again to invent another possibility for my writing to you. You mustn't go to the post office in vain, even your little postman – who is he? – mustn't do it, nor should even the postmistress be asked unnecessarily. If you can find no other possibility, then one must put up with it, but at least make a little effort to find one. Last night I dreamed about you. What happened in detail I can hardly remember, all I know is that we kept merging into one another. I was you, you were me. Finally you somehow caught fire. Remembering that one extinguished fire with clothing, I took an old coat and beat you with it. But again the transmutations began and it went so far that you were no longer even there, instead it was I who was on fire and it was also I who beat the fire with the coat. But the beating didn't help and it only confirmed my old fear that such things can't extinguish a fire. In the meantime, however, the fire brigade arrived and somehow you were saved. But you were different from before, spectral, as though drawn with chalk against the dark, and you fell, lifeless or perhaps having fainted from joy at having been saved, into my arms. But here too the uncertainty of transmutability entered, perhaps it was I who fell into someone's arms.[10]

The dreams are of her body, a fantasy body more real than its fleshly self: 'I see you more clearly, the movements of your body, your hands, so quick, so determined, it's almost a meeting, although when I try to raise my eyes to your face, what breaks into the flow of the letter . . .

is fire and I see nothing but fire.' But the fire does not extend to the sexual. That aspect of their relationship, 'the half-hour in bed – men's business', as she calls it, is evidently a horror for Kafka. He bemoans (and relishes) the fact that 'we shall never live together, in the same apartment, body to body, at the same table, never, not even in the same town.'[11] Kafka was living in July 1920 in Elli's apartment. Milena remained safely in Vienna. For the moment, according to her letters to Brod, Kafka's illness was not the barrier, but an unceasing anxiety about the flesh. They met again in mid-August at the new Austria-Czech border at Gmünd for a day. Kafka was exhausted; when he returned to Prague his physician ordered him to go to a specialized tuberculosis sanatorium. Kafka abjured, fearing the meat-eating, injection culture of such sanatoria, 'where beard-stroking Jewish doctors, as callous toward Jew as Christian look on.'[12] The tuberculosis sanatoria with their reliance on 'modern medicine' (and their rational Jewish doctors) were so very different from the world of the 'health cure' that he desired.

Kafka's life was now spent wandering between institutions. In December 1920 he was in Matliary in the High Tatra of Slovakia for a rest cure; he remained there on leave until August 1921. He assumed that the clientele was primarily non-Jewish, but quickly learned that the social segregation extended into the mountains and that most of his fellow guests too were Jews. He undertook the 'rest cure' that was standard for tuberculosis: a version of Weir Mitchell's rest cure for neurasthenia and hysteria, requiring much rich (vegetarian) food, lots of milk and enforced inaction. Franz continued his exchange with Milena who, however, was now convinced that his anxiety made any transformative cure impossible. The young Hungarian-Jewish physician Robert Klopstock also suffered from tuberculosis. Both he and Franz were reading Kierkegaard, and they became friends over their shared interest. Klopstock began to care for him. In mid-August Franz wrote to his superior in Prague:

At the sanatorium in Matliary, where Kafka stayed from December 1920 to August 1921. Kafka is in the first row; his friend the physician Robert Klopstock is in the back row, middle.

I am writing this letter in bed. I wanted to return to Prague on the 19th of this month, but I am afraid that it won't be possible. For several months I have been almost free of fever, but on Sunday I woke up with a fever, which climbed to over 38 degrees and still continues today. It's probably not the result of a cold, but one of those chance things common to lung disease, which one cannot avoid. The doctor who examined me and found my lungs to be in good condition except for a stubborn remnant considers this acute fever to have little significance. Nonetheless, I still have to stay in bed while the fever persists. Hopefully, the fever will disappear by Friday, then I would get underway; otherwise I would have to stay several days longer, in which case I would bring with me a doctor's report. This fever, from which I suffer a considerable loss of body weight anyway, is for me even sadder because it prevents me after such a long holiday from fulfilling even the minimal duty of appearing for work on time.

He returned to work on 29 August 1921 having gained less than twenty pounds. His letters to Milena continued, reflecting now on the impossibility of any true relationship with a woman: 'Evidently on account of my dignity, on account of my pride (no matter how humble he looks, the devious West European Jew!), I can only love what I can place so high above me that I can not reach it.'[13] Here is Franz caught between sets of obligations that are both demanding and transforming. Living again with his parents, escape seemed unlikely.

In spite (or because) of the turmoil in Kafka's life, he returned to writing, producing a series of short stories, many of which reflect on his 'anxiety' and his illness. The four tales, 'First Suffering', 'A Little Woman', 'A Hunger Artist' and 'Josephine, the Singer', are collected in a volume to be entitled *The Hunger Artist*. All of these stories reflect tropes about illness and death that are present in his earlier work and yet take on the double awareness of Kafka's own experience of tuberculosis. The title story is rooted in the reality of there having been circus sideshow acts known as 'geeks', who would starve themselves and then be put on show to prove that they were not eating. As Kafka opens the tale:

> During these last decades the interest in professional fasting has markedly diminished. It used to pay very well to stage such great performances under one's own management, but today that is quite impossible. We live in a different world now. At one time the whole town took a lively interest in the hunger artist; from day to day of his fast the excitement mounted; everybody wanted to see him at least once a day; there were people who bought season tickets for the last few days and sat from morning till night in front of his small barred cage.[14]

But here the starving body of the 'artist' is revealed not to be the product of self-control, of artistry, but merely the product of necessity. The tale ends with the artist being discovered abandoned and still starving in his cage well after any interest in such art forms has waned:

> 'Are you still fasting?' asked the overseer, 'when on earth do you mean to stop?' 'Forgive me, everybody,' whispered the hunger artist; only the overseer, who had his ear to the bars, understood him. 'Of course,' said the overseer, and tapped his forehead with a finger to let the attendants know what state the man was in, 'we forgive you.' 'I always wanted you to admire my fasting,' said the hunger artist. 'We do admire it,' said the overseer, affably. 'But you shouldn't admire it,' said the hunger artist. 'Well then we don't admire it,' said the overseer, 'but why shouldn't we admire it?' 'Because I have to fast, I can't help it,' said the hunger artist. 'What a fellow you are,' said the overseer, 'and why can't you help it?' 'Because,' said the hunger artist, lifting his head a little and speaking, with his lips pursed, as if for a kiss, right into the overseer's ear, so that no syllable might be lost, 'because I couldn't find the food I liked. If I had found it, believe me, I should have made no fuss and stuffed myself like you or anyone else.'[15]

'A Hunger Artist' reproduces much of the anxiety about confinement, exposure, the spectacle and emaciation of the body, and about becoming what one was fated to become by projecting it onto the social reality of the hunger artists who actually functioned as carnival geeks at the turn of the century. The anxiety becomes a positive quality that suffuses the entire narrative, and yet one can read in this reversal all of the anxiety that Kafka repressed. For Kafka's geek turns out in the end to have been a freak – he has no real control over his actions, he must become what he is fated to become, a hunger artist. Here Kafka evokes a ritual of starvation not through the agency of the artist but because of a programmed capacity of the artist's body over which he has no control. This is the problem with Gregor Samsa's diet – and perhaps also that of Kafka himself. It is a specific form of anorexia nervosa from which this figure suffers, fashioned by the dictates of his body and his mind as understood by the culture in which he lived. His body manifests the predisposition of the Jewish or tubercular body for disease. The claustrophobic sense of inevitability is heightened by its ending. The death of the protagonist and his replacement in his now cleaned cage by a panther evokes the heart of Rainer Marie Rilke's poem 'The Panther in the Paris Zoo' (1907), where the panther's eyes open: 'from time to time the pupil's shutter / Will draw apart: an image enters then, / To travel through the tautened body's utter / Stillness – and in the heart to end.' Kafka's story was an immediate hit. In the November 1921 issue of the *Neue Rundschau* an article had appeared on 'The Writer Franz Kafka', with the promise that something new by this writer would soon appear. In the summer of 1922 Kafka sent 'The Hunger Artist' to its editor, Rudolf Kayser.

At the beginning of January 1922 Kafka experienced a 'nervous breakdown' that seems to have completely debilitated him. One of his physicians had already suggested a rest cure for the tuberculosis, which he had begun on 29 October 1921. To further recuperate he travelled in January 1922 to Spindelrmühle (now Špindlerův Mlýn), near the Polish border, where Kafka again began to write a novel, reading the first section to Brod on 15 March. The evening he arrived in the mountains he wrote in his diary of 'the strange, mysterious, perhaps dangerous, perhaps redeeming consolation of writing'. Two great novel fragments already existed: *Amerika* and *The Trial*. On 1 July he officially received his pension. By then the first chapters of *The Castle* had been written.

In a complex way the tale of the land surveyor Josef K. is an elaborate recapitulation of Kafka's parable 'Before the Law'. K.

arrives in the village late in the evening in the dead of winter seem-ingly hired by the authorities at the Castle, but he cannot even see the Castle from the inn where he stays. He learns in ever more complex ways that the Castle is a hierarchy of bureaucrats, with sub- and sub-sub-stewards and their assistants all standing between him and the Count Westwest, who may have hired him. When day comes he can see what he takes to be the Castle – just a jumbled collection of crumbling stone houses and a tower. When he asks about being allowed to enter the Castle he is told in one breath that that will never be permitted. Immediately afterward a messenger from the Castle, Barnabas, shows up and gives K. a letter from Klamm, a Castle official, which says that he has indeed been accepted and should report to the Council Chairman, who will tell him his duties.

Klamm seems to be the powerful representative of the Castle, at least in the inn. His mistress Frieda seduces K. and he promises to marry her. But marriage is the least of K.'s problems. He is told that the job of land surveyor had been announced decades ago. Even then one was not needed, but the file had been lost, and the case became mired in the Castle bureaucracy, bouncing between different departments. And yet K. notes that it had been confirmed the night he arrived that there was a job at the Castle for him.

The longer K. waits the less likely it seems that he will be employed, or even that he will be able to speak to someone who knows anything about his employment. The unlikelihood of this is proven when he receives a letter telling him how happy the Castle is with the work K. has done as land surveyor, and also with the assistants' work, and that he should continue his good work. K.'s life revolves around Frieda and his search for a way of entering the Castle. His life with Frieda is hampered by her own anxiety that K. stays with her only on account of her relationship to Klamm and his hope that this will lead to him being given access to the Castle. Eventually K. abandons Frieda, who returns to her original job at the inn. K's search is unending. He seeks after one bureaucrat named Erlanger, only to discover behind one of the innumerable doors a man named Bürgel, who, in a parody of Austrian official-speak, tells K. that, instead of waiting for your case to pass through the official channels, which could take forever, it is possible to get your case taken care of by accidentally wandering into the room of another official who is able to help you, and he won't be able to refuse you. But of course this can never be. K. wanders back to the inn and in a sense begins his search over again. Kafka told his friend Max Brod how the novel would end: K., exhausted from his fruitless quest to enter the Castle, would be on his deathbed, around which the villagers gather. As he is dying he gets a message from the Castle stating that, although K.'s claims to staying in the village are not valid, nevertheless, taking into account the circumstances, he would be allowed to live and work there. Much like the close of 'Before the Law' this announcement would come too late and would only provide the ultimate sense of fruitlessness for the search for meaning in life and work.

The isolation of *The Castle*, and K.'s impossible struggle to attain access to it, is a simple reversal of the anxiety and attraction of the sanatorium. Kafka, who spent every possible vacation as an adult visiting health spas, knew of the attraction of being treated as a patient even when one's illnesses were psychosomatic. The placebo effect of living as a voluntary patient carried with it a *frisson* of being ill while not being ill. How different it was when one was truly ill, when the choice of coming and going was no longer one's own. It is important to understand that compulsory notification and compulsory treatment for tuberculosis come to be a reality in Austria and Czechoslovakia only at the very moment when Kafka himself was ill. *The Castle* represents a world with heightened and focused sexuality, which is parallel to the medical myths of the sanatorium echoed in Thomas Mann's contemporary novel *The*

Magic Mountain (1924), based on Mann's visit to the famed Swiss Davos sanatorium for just four weeks from 15 May to 12 June 1912 (and a wide range of tuberculosis literature from the period). It was a 'modern' sanatorium after the model of Hermann Brehmer's fresh-air hospital for tuberculosis patients founded in 1854. Such hospitals with their rest cure quickly became known as places of debauchery, much like Kafka's image – not of the Castle – but of the inn where K. lodges. For Kafka's sanatoria were often inns or 'rest homes' rather than fully fledged, doctor-run sanatoria. K.'s is a world framed by a sense of the impossibility of entrance (escape) but the focused desire to access (escape) the confines of the Castle. Indeed, the very physical presence of the Castle looming on the hill overlooking the inn and the village suggests the isolation of the 'modern' sanatorium, which had become the site of cure for Kafka's world.

Kafka more and more saw himself as unable to enter the Castle – whatever that might have meant to him. It is clear that one meaning was the society to which he felt he belonged and which quickly turned against him. In 1922 Kafka read Hans Blüher's pamphlet on this topic, *Secessio Judaica* (1922). Blüher (1888–1955) had once been an advocate of Freud, but he had broken over Freud's Jewishness and was a strong advocate of the German Youth Movement with all of its homoerotic overtones. By the 1920s he was an implacable anti-Semite. On 15 March 1922 Kafka notes: 'Objections to be made against the book: he has popularized it, and with a will, moreover – and with magic. How he escapes the dangers (Blüher).'[16] And then Kafka tries to write an answer to Blüher:

16 June 1922. Quite apart from the insuperable difficulties always presented by Blüher's philosophical and visionary power, one is in the difficult position of easily incurring the suspicion, almost with one's every remark, of wanting ironically to dismiss the ideas of this book. One is suspect even if, as in my case, there is

nothing further from one's mind, in the face of this book, than irony. This difficulty in reviewing his book has its counterpart in a difficulty that Blüher, from his side, cannot surmount. He calls himself an anti-Semite without hatred, *sine ira et studio*, and he really is that; yet he easily awakens the suspicion, almost with his every remark, that he is an enemy of the Jews, whether out of happy hatred or out of unhappy love. These difficulties confront each other like stubborn facts of nature, and attention must be called to them lest in reflecting on this book one stumble over these errors and at the very outset be rendered incapable of going on. According to Blüher, one cannot refute Judaism inductively, by statistics, by appealing to experience; these methods of the older anti-Semitism cannot prevail against Judaism; all other peoples can be refuted in this way, but not the Jews, the chosen people; to each particular charge the anti-Semites make, the Jew will be able to give a particular answer in justification. Blüher makes a very superficial survey, to be sure, of the particular charges and the answers given them. This perception, insofar as it concerns the Jews and not the other peoples, is profound and true. Blüher draws two conclusions from it, a full and a partial one.[17]

Kafka's comments break off at this point. Unable to proceed, Kafka wrote on 30 June 1922 to his friend Dr Robert Klopstock:

Secessio Judaica. Won't you write something about it? I cannot do it; when I try, my hand immediately goes dead, even though I, like everyone else, would have a great deal to say about it. Somewhere in my ancestry I too must have a Talmudist, I should hope, but he does not embolden me enough to go ahead, so I set you to it. It does not have to be a refutation, only an answer to the appeal. That ought to be very tempting. And there is indeed a temptation to let one's flock graze on this

German and yet not entirely alien pasture, after the fashion of the Jews.[18]

Here Kafka mimics the rhetoric of the early Freudian Blüher, an Aryan arguing like a Jew, yet stresses his own Jewishness against Blüher's hypocritical 'Germanness'. This 'Germanness' is one, however, shared by Kafka and Klopstock; it is 'not entirely alien pasture'. Blüher's case, according to Kafka, is one of a 'happy hatred or . . . unhappy love' that Blüher feels for the Jews, embodied in his 'very superficial survey, to be sure, of the particular charges and the answers given them'.

What is unstated in Kafka's dismissal of the 'very superficial survey, to be sure, of the particular charges and the answers given them', is that Blüher stresses the superficiality of the Jew's Westernization. For Blüher, the Jews remain the 'Orientals', no matter how they seem to have physically transformed. They regress to what they always have been, once they are removed from Western society. Blüher's text evokes in a powerful manner the idea of a Jewish racial type: 'The Jews are the only people that practise mimicry. Mimicry of the blood, of the name, and of the body.'[19] Here Blüher simply picks up the rhetoric of 'scientific' thinkers of the time such as Werner Sombart, who argued in *The Jews and Modern Capitalism* (1911) that the Jewish body is inherently immutable. Sombart's notion of the immutable does not contradict his image of Jewish mimicry; for him, the Jew represents immutable mutability:

The driving power in Jewish adaptability is of course the idea of a purpose, or a goal, as the end of all things. Once the Jew has made up his mind what line he will follow, the rest is comparatively easy, and his mobility only makes his success more sure. How mobile the Jew can be is positively astounding. He is able to give himself the personal appearance he most desires . . . The best illustrations may be drawn from the United States, where the Jew of the second or third generation is with more difficulty distinguished from the non-Jew. You can tell the German after no matter how many generations; so with the Irish, the Swede, the Slav. But the Jew, in so far as his racial features allow it, has been successful in imitating the Yankee type, especially in regard to outward marks such as clothing, bearing, and the peculiar method of hairdressing.[20]

For Blüher, as for Sombart, the Jewish mindset persists, though their bodies (and hairstyle) seem to be changing. Transformation is possible, Josef K. may strive for the Castle, but the end result is that all remains as it has always been no matter how the surface changes. The corrupt materialistic thought of the Jews disrupts those among whom they dwell by generating ideas that seem universal, yet are inherently Jewish. And 'the Jew Freud' and his notion of psychosomatic correlates represent only the most modern version of such corrosive Jewish thought.[21] It is to be found already in Spinoza's *Ethics*, and it is the identity of body and spirit. For Spinoza, as for Freud, when something occurs in the body it is because it occurs in the spirit. 'Where ever spirit is there is also body. Every idea has a corporeal correlate.'[22] The identity of mind and body, a central theme in Kafka's understanding of himself and his illness, is merely a Jewish 'trick' to get Aryans to believe that their *Geist* (spirit) and their bodies are crassly, materialistically linked. What seems to be a 'neutral' model of argumentation, the model of psychosomatic illness, is revealed to Kafka as 'Jewish'. Even that, his last refuge, is breached by the anti-Semites.

On 17 April 1922 Kafka asked to extend his leave from work, which he had been spending at his parent's apartment, writing and attempting to recuperate. By 7 June his health had so deteriorated that he asked again to retire and was finally granted his wish. On 1 July 1922 he left his life as a Czech civil servant. He moves to Planá, the village along the Luschnitz River where Ottla now lived. Here he continued to work on the manuscript of *The Castle*. Eventually he turned the incomplete and often confusing manuscript over to Milena for safe-keeping.

In July 1923 Kafka decided to take a vacation from all of this and went with his sister Elli and her children to a rest home at Müritz on the Baltic. He found himself there observing a group of 'Eastern European Jews whom West European Jews are rescuing from the dangers of Berlin. Half the days and nights the house, the woods, and the beach are filled with singing. I am not happy when I'm among them, but on the threshold of happiness.'[23] This summer camp had been created by Siegfried Lehmann, one of the leaders of Jewish education in Berlin, to bring inner city Eastern European Jewish children from the *Scheunenviertel*, the Jewish immigrant neighbourhood in the middle of the city, out into the healthy countryside. Such 'preventoria' were intended to decrease the number of cases of tuberculosis in the inner city. The children Kafka saw there were 'healthy, cheerful, blue-eyed children', according to a letter to Max Brod,[24] but they were also 'Hebrew-speaking, healthy, and cheerful',[25] according to a simultaneous letter to Robert Klopstock. Kafka reached the threshold of happiness observing this summer camp.

These Yiddish-speaking children, who were learning Hebrew at camp, provided Kafka with an indirect introduction to one of their counsellors, the 25-year-old Dora Dymant (also spelled Diamant) (1898–1952). From a small town near Łódź in central Poland, she had been raised in the penumbra of the court of the *Gerer rebbe*, the mystical leader of the Hasidic sect founded in Ger by Rabbi Isaac Meir in the mid-nineteenth century. Dora's father was the head of their synagogue in B´dzin. As a result, she spoke Yiddish as her mother tongue. She also knew Hebrew well because of her engagement with the Zionist youth group in Bédzin, a movement opposed by her father and much of Hasidic orthodoxy. As a young woman she was enrolled in the first Orthodox school for girls in Kraków but fled from there to Breslau, where she became fully involved with the secular world and learned German.

In the summer of 1923 Dora was employed by Siegfried Lehmann's Jewish People's Home in Berlin as a counsellor. Franz had suggested in 1916 that Felice should volunteer there when he was trying to convince her of his commitment to her and his newly found commitment to a Jewish identity. Felice Bauer never volunteered and more importantly she became part of a calculus of sexual politics that Max Brod had made explicit in his 'Letter to a Galician School Girl', published in Buber's *The Jew* in 1916: 'Our Western Jewesses are either shallow and superficial or else . . . they fall into nervousness, testiness, conceit, despair, isolation . . . Galician girls as a whole are so much fresher, more spiritually substantial, and healthier than our girls.'[26] Dora was the promised cure for Franz, she would bring her Eastern health to cure him of his own Western nervousness. In fantasy at least she was the cure for the illness that was named Felice, but was actually Franz's very own.

At the beginning of August Dora met Franz at a Sabbath evening meal. Soon the intensity of the relationship was such that the two imagined a future life that would eventually move from an interim stop in Berlin towards her dream, Palestine. All would be healthy and productive – answers to two of the standard complaints of their world against the Jews: that they were sickly and parasitic. In Palestine she would be a cook and Franz fantasized about working there as a waiter. If Dora was a new medicine then Berlin was to be Kafka's antidote against Prague, as he had written in September 1922 to Robert Klopstock: 'Since the Western European Jew is a sick man and lives on medicines, it is essential for him . . . not to pass up Berlin.'[27] Dymant was Kafka's last great love and his last attempt to heal himself.

Later in August Kafka stopped off in Berlin on his way back to Prague from Müritz. He had gained some weight on his vacation and confronted his parents when he returned to Prague, spending

Dora Dymant, Kafka's last love, who called herself Mrs Kafka after Franz's death.

'one of the very worst nights'[28] of his life the evening he left his parents' home. Berlin offered much – not the least being the distance from Prague. But Germany also offered a better financial situation, since the exploding German inflation meant nothing if you had hard currency such as the Czech kronen. There was also a more complex type of Jewish community, with such organizations as the Institute for the Science of the Jews (Hochschule für die Wissenschaft des Judentums), founded in 1870, where Kafka was to study. After staying with Ottla in Schelesen for a month, he returned to Berlin on 24 September 1923 and took an apartment in the bedroom community of Steglitz. He quickly moved on, steadily moving towards the green fringes of the city. In November he was in Grunewald and then, being unable to keep up the rent, at the beginning of February 1924 in Zehlendorf, both lush, green suburbs. Berlin was a major break from family, from Prague, and even from his own earlier writings. But he regularly wrote to his parents assuring them of his ever-improving health and enquiring after his nieces' and nephews' Jewish education. He wrote to a Swiss publisher who asked to publish something new for a rather substantial amount. He felt that all his earlier writings were no longer useful. He was slowly reading a Hebrew novel, Josef Chaim Brenner's *Loss and Stumble*, a page a day. Dora was the embodiment of everything that he wanted: she was political and mystical, religious and secular, German and yet also Hebrew with a touch of Yiddish for spice, feminine and devoted: at least in his eyes. He wrote short story after story in the late afternoons and evenings and focused everything on Dora.

The stories echo his own sense of his new world of illness and of isolation, even as he is engaged in building an ever more intense relationship with Dora. One night he wrote until dawn and the next day read her the tale of 'The Burrow'. This belongs to a nameless animal who finds a haven, fashioned with its own blood: 'I was glad when the blood came, for that was proof that the walls were beginning to harden; and in that way, as everybody must admit, I richly paid for my Castle Keep.'[29] The inhabitant of this blood-soaked castle can sleep only 'beneath the moss on the top of my bloodstained spoil'.[30] Even its own death would not be pointless in this protected warren: 'even in my enemy's mortal stroke at the final hour, for my blood will ebb away here in my own soil and not be lost'.[31] Blood as a sign of purification, as in the ritual slaughter engaged in by his own grandfather, mixes with its perversion and misreading in the debates about how Jews were accused of ritual murder, using the blood of Christians, as well as with the blood of Kafka's own experience of tuberculosis, to

Kafka's last portrait in 1923.

provide a frame for this 'Castle Keep'. Now, locked into rather than out of the Castle, Kafka seeks solace in his confinement. Its location is unstated but Dora knew that it was in Berlin.

Kafka's health collapsed. Poor, robbed of even the advantage of his pension in Czech kronen by the end of the galloping inflation in Germany, his friends from Prague visited him regularly. Indeed by this point Hermann was sending his prodigal son money to supplement his pension. In January 1924 Dora and Franz were down to heating their meals over candle stubs. Ottla came at the end of February. His uncle Siegfried Löwy, the 'country doctor', visited him in Zehlendorf at the end of February and determined that he was in need of medical supervision. In early March Max Brod came to Berlin for the premiere of his translation of the libretto of Janáček's *Jenufa* and saw how poorly Franz was doing. On 17 March Brod took him back to Prague and Dora followed soon after. Staying with his parents, it became clear that the tuberculosis was spreading. By the beginning of April he had been admitted to the 'Wienerwald' sanatorium in Ortmann, Lower Austria, where his tuberculosis of the lungs was diagnosed as having spread into his larynx. He was mute. He weighed little more than 45 kilograms. He communicated with his visitors by means of a notepad, like the deaf Beethoven. It was a fate that he had earlier abhorred in a letter to Max Brod on 11 March 1921:

I am firmly convinced, now that I have been living here among consumptives, that healthy people run no danger of infection. Here, however, the healthy are only the woodcutters in the forest and the girls in the kitchen (who will simply pick uneaten food from the plates of patients and eat it – patients whom I shrink from sitting opposite) but not a single person from our town circles. But how loathsome it is to sit opposite a larynx patient, for instance (blood brother of a consumptive but far sadder), who sits across from you so friendly and harmless, looking at you with the transfigured eyes of the consumptive and at the same time coughing into your face through his spread fingers drops of purulent phlegm from his tubercular ulcer. At home I would be sitting that way, though not quite in so a dire state, as 'good uncle' among the children.[32]

On 10 April 1924 Kafka was transferred to the clinic of the laryngologist Markus Hajek, whose botched operation on Sigmund Freud's cancerous jaw in April 1923 almost killed him. Hajek's records focus on the profound destruction that the infection had caused within the body. It became more and more difficult to drink or eat. Dora was constantly at his side. Kafka was in a ward and became increasingly depressed as his own condition weakened and others in the ward died one by one and were silently removed. Brod, still in Prague, was appalled by Dora's account of Kafka's state and asked Franz Werfel, with whom Kafka had quarrelled, to intervene to get him a private room. Werfel was the best known of the Prague writers but Kafka felt that his play *Schweiger* demeaned the memory of Otto Gross (and Kafka's own struggle with his own father). Werfel did intervene and sent Franz roses and an inscribed copy of his new bestseller, *Verdi*, which Kafka read with great pleasure during his few waking hours. Hajek was dismissive of such gestures and refused Kafka any special treatment. 'A certain Werfel has written me that I should do something for a certain Kafka', he notes, 'I know who Kafka is. He is the patient in number 12. But who is Werfel?'

Dora and his friends were appalled by Hajek's callous treatment and arranged to have him transferred to the Kierling Sanatorium near Klosterneuburg, not thirty minutes from Vienna, where at least he could get some more personal care. On 19 April he and Dora moved to the small sanatorium of Dr Hugo Hoffmann. There the physicians provided palliative care for Franz. He read proofs of *A Hunger Artist* and altered the order of the stories; this was to be published posthumously by the Zionist-Marxist publishing house Verlag die Schmiede in Berlin. By the end of May Kafka was demanding that his friend Robert Klopstock, who remained there with Dora, should increase the dosages of morphine, just as Sigmund

Freud would ask on 21 September 1939. Similarly, as Max Schur, Freud's physician, would do, Klopstock had promised Franz that if things became unbearable he would give him an overdose of the drug. Kafka whispered to him: 'Kill me, or else you are a murderer.'

At noon on Tuesday, 2 June 1924, Franz Kafka died of tuberculosis as Robert Klopstock held his head. He was buried on 11 June, the first to be placed in the family burial plot in the new Jewish cemetery in Strašnice, in the suburbs of Prague: not the ancient burial place of the Prague Jews in the centre of the old Ghetto, haunted by the ghost of Rabbi Löw, the creator of the Golem, but the middle-class, grassy slopes of the new Jewish Prague to which Kafka had truly belonged for good or for ill. Dora fainted at the graveside. A week after the burial a memorial service was held in Prague attended by more than 500 people. On 5 June Milena had published an obituary in Czech, evoking Kafka as 'a man condemned to regard the world with such blinding clarity that he found it unbearable and went to his death'. With Kafka's death his legend really began.

4

A Life after Life

Max Brod was appointed Kafka's literary executor by the terms of Kafka's two undated wills. In both of these he was admonished to destroy the unpublished work and to see the completed work of Kafka's final years, such as 'Josephine, the Singer', through to publication. Brod collected the unpublished manuscripts, including the diaries that Kafka had given to Milena, except for the very last manuscripts and letters that Kafka left with Dora. These were eventually seized by the Nazis and vanished. After Kafka's death Brod undertook one of the greatest acts of literary impiety and one of the most valuable ones of literary and cultural history. He refused to follow Kafka's wishes and began to publish Kafka's works in their entirety. In 1925 he persuaded the avant-garde Berlin publisher Verlag die Schmiede to bring out *The Trial*; Kurt Wolff published *The Castle* in 1926 and *Amerika* in 1927.

Kafka's work began to appear in other languages, as well as German: there were Czech and Hungarian translations of some of the shorter prose, a Spanish and then a French translation of 'The Metamorphosis' appeared in the late 1920s. English editions began with Edwin and Willa Muir's translation of *The Castle* in 1930. While these projects had only a critical success Brod planned a 'Collected Edition' with the Gustav Kiepenheuer publishing house, which was abandoned when the Nazis seized power in 1933. The Nazis, in a fit of 'political correctness', claimed early on that they wished only to separate the Jews from the German body politic (echoing Blüher's views) and provide them with a shadow culture, the Jewish Cultural League: Jewish theatres, symphony orchestras and publishing houses to produce a 'Jewish' culture only for the consumption of the Jews. Brod asked the German-Jewish department-store magnate Salman Schocken (1877–1959) and his Schocken Press to undertake the Kafka edition. Schocken had funded Buber's *The Jew* in 1915, the writings of Franz Rosenzweig and, after World War I, sponsored the fiction of Shmuel Yosef Czaczkes, a young Galician-born Hebrew writer living in Germany, who was to win the Nobel Prize as S. J. Agnon. Kafka seemed a natural addition to this attempt to construct a new Jewish High Culture but Lambert Schneider, Schocken's chief editor, felt that his work was beyond the official mandate of the Jewish Cultural League. Schneider was ignored and a small anthology, *Before the Law*, appeared in 1934. Brod asked the Jewish nationalist Hans-Joachim Schoeps to aid him; when they differed radically about the specific implications of Zionism for Kafka, he turned to the young Viennese poet Hans Politzer. The volumes began to appear in Berlin and then in Prague. After the Nazi seizure of power the Kafka edition continued from Prague. The Nazis quickly put Kafka on the list of 'harmful and undesirable writing'. Schocken's publishing house was closed in 1939.

With the gradual posthumous publication of Kafka's works he became an exemplary figure for the modern condition – no matter how defined. His reputation was as much a litmus test for his contemporaries' sense of their world as he desired his texts to be: hermetic but transparent, revealing only a mirror underneath. Walter Benjamin (1892–1940), a thinker equally difficult to decipher, saw Kafka as espousing the horrors of a life made unusual because 'everything continues as usual'. For Benjamin, in his essay 'Franz Kafka: On the Tenth Anniversary of his Death', this is the eternal 'catastrophe', and is the 'Kafka-like situation'. Suddenly Kafka becomes a brand name for an era. But the era had already absorbed Kafka's sense of alienation, stemming from his complex position as Jew, German-speaker, son of Central Europe and son of the Kafkas and the Löwys, without Kafka present. In 1923 Wallace Stevens, the American Protestant poet and insurance executive, in the concluding stanza of his 'Tea at the Palaz of Hoon' evokes a world to which the dying Kafka completely subscribed:

I was the world in which I walked, and what I saw
Or heard or felt came not but from myself;
And there I found myself more truly and more strange.

This is the world of the Kafkaesque already present but needing a name.

The brand name Kafka came to be used for many products. Benjamin's foil Gershom Scholem (1897–1982) saw in him a Jewish mystic beyond mysticism, just as he later saw Benjamin in much the same role. Scholem later took seriously the claims of Sabbati Sevi, the seventeenth-century mystic who claimed to be the messiah, as a historical figure in terms of the intransigent feelings of his followers, who refused to acknowledge that his claim was false even after he converted to Islam; Scholem read Kafka as one of the 36 unknown seers and he remained one of his followers without question. Kafka's complex and conflicted relationship to the multiple models of Judaism and Jewry in his times is reduced to Kafka as Jewish philosopher. Toward the end of Scholem's article 'Ten Unhistorical Statements about the Kabbalah', written in the 1920s and financed by Salman Schocken, he writes: 'Although unaware of it himself, [Kafka's] writings are a secularized representation of the kabalistic conception of the world. This is why many of today's readers find something of the rigorous splendour of the canonical in them – a hint of the Absolute that breaks into pieces.' Kafka became the modern centrepiece of his widely influential study *Major Trends in Jewish Mysticism* (1941), which placed Kafka in the lineage of Jewish mystical thought. In his book on *Walter Benjamin: The Story of a Friendship*, Scholem quotes his own comment to Benjamin: 'I said then . . . that one would have to read the works of Franz Kafka before one could understand the Kabbalah today, and particularly *The Trial*.' A decade after Kafka's death, and at a point when his works had become part of a modernist canon, the entire modernist as well as Jewish tradition vanished as the Nazis attempted to destroy European Jewish culture. Not only did the Nazis burn books, Kafka's included, but, as Heinrich Heine sagely observed a century before, those who burn books also burn people. Among those who died in the death camps were Kafka's three sisters as well as Grete Bloch and Milena Jesenská-Pollak.

Kafka's work continued to appear in English, when Schocken relocated his press in 1940 to New York City with Hannah Arendt and Nahum Glatzer as his chief editors. Most of the reviews of his work before his death had appeared in Prague; as with his smaller works, they were read by a rather limited circle of high modernist readers. His work was reviewed, but often by his Prague friends such as Max Brod, Otto Pick or Felix Weltsch. His reputation was solid but limited – a writer in a minor language, a term he himself coined. With the extensive publication of Kafka in English, and then in 1951 with the republication of the Brod edition by S. Fischer in Frankfurt (an older German-Jewish house that re-established itself after the war), Kafka went mainstream. As Hannah Arendt wrote to Salman Schocken on 9 August 1946: 'Though during his lifetime he could not make a decent living, he will now keep generations of intellectuals both gainfully employed and well-fed.'

After the Communists seized Czechoslovakia in 1948, Kafka was again exiled from Prague. In the eyes of Marxist critics behind the Iron Curtain Kafka was an exemplary bourgeois writer (and they were quite right about this). Bertolt Brecht evoked this in his 1934 essay on 'modern Czechoslovakian Literature', in which he acknowledged that Kafka is worth studying to see how he foretold the

'Dantesque' making of the concentration camps. Remember that the first camp, Dachau, was opened only in March 1933. With the 1963 conference at Liblice, organized by Eduard Goldstücker, Kafka became a political icon. This conference heralded the Prague Spring that vanished along with the new political Kafka in 1968. These political writers of the Prague Spring understood, as Philip Roth has recently commented in the *New York Times Book Review* (19 September 2004), that 'they were wilfully violating the integrity of Kafka's implacable imagination, though they went ahead nonetheless – and with all their might – to exploit his books to serve a political purpose during a horrible national crisis.' But this is of course the inherent flexibility that Kafka planned into his works and that all readers have exploited. Kafka became a sign for the Czech writer of resistance of the alien, as Miroslav Holub writes in his poem 'Jewish cemetery at Olsany, Kafka's grave, April, a sunny day':

Searching under the sycamores
are some words poured out from language.
Loneliness skin-tight
and therefore stony.
The old man by the gate,
looking like Gregor Samsa
but unmetamorphosed,
squints in this
naked light
and answers every question:
I'm sorry, I don't know.
I'm a stranger here.

In France it is Albert Camus (1913–1960), rereading Kafka's account of illness, death, and the collapse of belief in his novel *The Plague* (1947), who makes Kafka into an existentialist, even an absurdist. If Kafka's work, especially his story of 'The Penal Colony', can be taken as an extended fantasy on the case of Dreyfus and his imprisonment, Camus' plague infestation of Oran powerfully evokes the Nazis' capture of France. Camus had used dozens of references to Kafka, especially to *The Trial* and *The Castle*, as almost his point of origin of the sense of isolation and despair in *The Myth of Sisyphus* (1942). This extraordinary commentary on abandonment, written in occupied France, outlined his notion of the absurd and of its acceptance with 'the total absence of hope, which has nothing to do with despair, a continual refusal, which must not be confused with renunciation – and a conscious dissatisfaction.' Kafka is part of Camus' archaeology of culture, including Balzac, Sade, Melville, Stendhal, Dostoyevsky, Proust and Malraux, into which Camus places his own work. Kafka has become by 1942 a canonical writer of the modern, as André Gide notes in his diaries from the 1940s. In England the Austrian-born philosopher Ludwig Wittgenstein is reading Kafka against that grain, seeing him simply among those believers who refuse a belief in a personal God.

All of these appropriations strip Kafka of any specific identity as a Jew. Given the extraordinary moment in which Kafka is made into the 'exemplary modern man', the fact that his Jewish identity is removed is of importance. Jean-Paul Sartre would argue in his *Anti-Semite and Jew* (1946) that societies create their own Jews through the discourse of anti-Semitism. Otherwise Jews cannot exist. Kafka is thus not a Jew because he is part of the canon of 'human' not 'Jewish' experience.

By the late 1940s and '50s Kafka is being read by Jorge Luis Borges (1899–1986), who translated bits of Kafka into Spanish and echoes him in much of his fiction. He discovered Kafka in his job as a cataloguer at the Miguel Cane branch of the Buenos Aires Municipal Library. The job did not interest him (much like Kafka's insurance job) and he usually disappeared into the basement to read, especially Kafka. His essay 'Kafka and his Precursors' was written in 1951 and evokes his notion of a world in which Kafka and Borges are part of the same world since 'every writer "creates" his own precursors. His work modifies our conception of the past, as it will modify the future.' Italo Calvino (1923–1985), in his *Invisible Cities*, rethinks Kafka's fantasy world: 'My author is Kafka, and my favourite novel is *Amerika*.' This is of little surprise in a writer of surreal fairy-tales. In none of these writers is Kafka any more than his texts. Little reflection is given to his cultural or personal identity, as all of these readers of Kafka need to place him in their own personal genealogy of writing.

Philip Roth (born 1933) in the United States turns to Kafka as the essential exemplar of a modern Jewish identity. In 'I Always Wanted You to Admire My Fasting, or, Looking at Kafka' (1973) he presents the tale in an intimate present tense, of Kafka's escape from family and guilt up to 1924, when on his deathbed he is correcting proofs for his story 'A Hunger Artist'. In the second half of the tale Roth tells of Kafka somehow surviving to become young Philip's Newark Hebrew teacher in 1942. When this Kafka dies, the obituary says, 'He leaves no survivors.' But, of course, Roth is one, as his entire work shows. His *Portnoy's Complaint* (1969) was, according to Roth, inspired by Kafka. But most clearly his own take upon 'The Metamorphosis' shows how he thinks about Kafka as a literary icon, much in the same manner as does Camus or Borges: his extraordinary novella *The Breast* (1972) is about the transformation of a man into a breast – a female breast.

One morning after a restless night David Kepesh, Professor of Comparative Literature at the State University of New York at Stony Brook, awakes to find himself transformed into 'a mammary gland such as could only appear, one would have thought, in a dream or a Dali painting' (p. 13). His doctors are puzzled at this transformation and have multiple explanations. It is 'a phenomenon that has been variously described as . . . "a massive hormonal influx", "an endocrinopathic catastrophe", and / or "a hermaphroditic explosion of chromosomes"' (p. 13). All of these explanations, we shall see in the rest of this chapter, come to be models for the rationale of why men have (not necessarily are) breasts.

According to his physicians, Kepesh's new form is at least attractive – 'my flesh is smooth and "youthful", and I am still a "Caucasian"' (p. 14). These are notes read as if from his medical chart, stated by his endocrinologist. The breast is beautiful and white (read: erotic) as this image follows the construction of racial as well as sexual identity in Roth's account of Kepesh's life. Pleasure and happiness seem to stand at the centre of Kepesh's life as well as at the centre of this novella. For Kepesh's fetishization of the female breast as the source of his erotic pleasure becomes his nightmare of pleasure. For this giant, 155-pound breast is the site of erotic pleasure. His nipple, massaged and sucked, provides him with orgasm after orgasm. This fantasy of being transformed into one's own object of desire and experiencing the pleasure that one imagines providing is a narcissistic form of identification with one's own sexuality. The pleasure, which he imagines the breasts of his female sexual partners receiving, is the pleasure that he himself receives.

Kepesh eventually comes up with his own explanation for this transformation. He has been teaching too much Franz Kafka, especially 'The Metamorphosis' (pp. 60, 65–6). He has gone mad and imagined himself transformed as their characters were transformed. He is mad and thus his transformation is 'merely' a delusion. 'Did fiction do this to me?' he asks (p. 81). His psychoanalyst tells him that such an explanation is avoiding the reality of his transformation and is certainly 'the way into madness' (p. 61). 'Hormones are hormones and art is art' (p. 81). The transformation is 'real', not merely in his psyche. His unhappiness lies in his body, not in his soul. His choice is clear: 'I am indeed a wholly authentic breast – or else . . . I am as mad as any man has ever been' (p. 75). The tale is a comment on the power of sexuality in the 'Age of Reason' to shape our very sense of our selves; but it is also a commentary on the problems and potential of the transformation promised to everyone in the Enlightenment and feared and relished by Kafka.

Philip Roth, that consummate American-Jewish writer, transforms Gregor Samsa into a giant breast, thus denying any 'Jewish' roots to this fable by that (for him) most Jewish of writers, Franz Kafka. In South Africa quite the opposite transformation takes place. Achmat Dangor's novella *Kafka's Curse* (1997) is set in South Africa before the election of 1994. The theme, like that of Philip Roth's *The Human Stain* (2000), is passing off one's colour, specifically a 'coloured' man passing as 'white' by becoming a 'Jew'. Roth's account of the transformation of an African American into a Jew places the Jew in contemporary America as the desirable category – a Gregor Samsa in reverse. Dangor's story is rooted in the ideology of a specific multicultural Diaspora, that of South Africa under apartheid, where Dangor was born in 1948. He was a member of the black cultural group Black Thoughts and banned for six years in the 1970s.

Dangor's novella is his literary fantasy of the meaning of multiculturalism projected back into the world of apartheid. The protagonist of the tale, Omar Khan, changes his name to Oscar Kahn because he was able to pass as 'white': 'I was fair, and why not, my grandmother was Dutch. This oppressive country had next-to-Nazis in government, yet had a place, a begrudged place but a place nevertheless, for Jews. Can you believe it? For that eternally persecuted race? Because they were white' (p. 23). The Jews of South Africa became 'white' only after the beginning of the twentieth century . They became white because they became a successful minority and had the economic clout to demand being labelled as 'white.' Thus in the Cape Colony in 1902 an 'Immigration Restriction Act' was passed in order to limit the immigration of people from the Indian sub-continent. Only 'Europeans' were to be given the privilege of immigration to South Africa. 'Europeans' were defined by the alphabet of the language they spoke. Yiddish, needless to say, was not accepted as a 'European' language. Since only languages written in the same alphabet as Afrikaans and English were 'white,' Hebrew became 'coloured'. The 'Hebrews' entered into the world of Southern Africa with its overwhelming Black population not as members of the privileged, hegemonic race – as 'white' – but as a marginal race, as 'coloured'. This view, was of course, very much in line with late nineteenth-century racial theory in Europe. Houston Stewart Chamberlain, Wagner's son-in-law and the most widely read popular racial theorist of the day in all of Europe, argued that the Jews were a mongrel race for having mixed with Blacks in their Alexandrian exile, and this fact could be read on their physiognomy.

Dangor's protagonist Oscar Kahn defines his 'whiteness' by moving into a white neighbourhood. He left the Indian township of Lenasia and moved to a Johannesburg suburb, passed as a Jew, and married Anna Wallace, who was of impeccable British ancestry. Kahn suffers from their anti-Semitism. 'Anna's mother hated me. I think she suspected even my Jewishness. Prejudice has unerring instincts' (p. 32). For Anna's friends he is a sexual object but not a potential husband because of his visible difference: Oscar is 'all brown bread and honey! Good enough for bed . . . but to marry?' (p. 11). Marriage and reproduction and the difficulty of passing are at the heart of this tale. Her friends know that he is different: '"Are you Indian?" . . . "No, the Kahn here is a good old Jewish name"' (31). *Nomen est omen*, but how does one become 'Jewish'?

Oscar is eventually employed as an architect by a Jewish architect. Meyer Lewis employs him, trains him, and slowly makes him over into a image of himself: 'In my dreams I often slit Meyer's bulbous throat and danced with naked feet in the pools of his hot blood . . . I began to hate his hybrid South African Yiddisher tongue, his sharp contemptuous eyes . . . Meyer was short and stocky' (pp. 24–5). Language and physicality defines the 'real' Jew in the tale. Meyer, like Oscar, is a successful Jew. Yet he is still marked by his linguistic and physical difference.

When Oscar buys a house in a white-only suburb it is a house marked in an odd way by his 'Jewishness'. When he courted Anna, she would watch him masturbate: '[Anna] was not surprised that I was circumcised; a Jewish custom after all' (p. 31). Moslem men, like Jewish men, are physically different. This difference becomes the stain that mars the image of Oscar's house in the white suburb. It is a 90-year-old house. Oscar insists that it cannot be altered in any way. It has an odd configuration. When you approach the front door you are confronted by: 'a strange fountain that stood in the centre of the path leading to the front door, forcing people to confront the sorrowful sight of a castrated David, his drooping stone penis broken at the tip like a child's pee-pee. *It was an integral part of the house's nature*, Oscar said' (p. 11). The fountain of the 'young boyish David had water piped up through his foot and out his penis. The piping was made of metal and it rusted. Over time the rust coloured the water until he appeared to be peeing blood' (p. 37). The ancient fantasy of male Jews bleeding regularly had been the origin of the idea of Jewish ritual murder from the early modern times to the present. Jewish men were believed to need Christian blood to 'heal' their bloody discharge. This view persisted into the late nineteenth century. It was raised again at the turn of the century in a powerfully written pamphlet by the Professor of Hebrew at the University in St Petersburg, Daniel Chwolson, as one of the rationales used to justify the blood libel. Chwolson notes that it was used to 'cure the diseases believed to be specifically those of the Jews', such as male menstruation. The house that Oscar occupies is a 'Jewish' house with its bleeding David. While Oscar is circumcised, as a Moslem he is not condemned to bleed.

The earlier inhabitant of the house, a little boy called Simon, was embarrassed by the blood-peeing David; he took a garden spade and 'lopped David's penis off' (p. 38). Again, in the Western image of the Jewish body, circumcision is a form of real or attenuated castration. The power of the image of Jewish circumcision in the West is such that it actually elides any reference to the practice by other peoples, such as the Muslims. When Oscar buys the house, one of his first tasks is to repair the statue and have it working again. It begins to pee blood again. Oscar believes that he probably tore the new plastic tube when he inserted it. His daughters read it differently: 'The girls blushed. The elder one said that David was peeing monthlies' (p. 38). Dangor makes an association between the Jewish body, here clearly not a white body, but a successful body nevertheless, and the myth-making inherent in Western society about Jewish physical difference. It was just as present in the legends of Jewish difference in southern Africa a hundred years before as it was in the Muslim propaganda concerning the Jews in the 1970s and '80s.

After Oscar dies his children discover that his mistress Elizabeth Marsden is a sculptress 'with a gift for pissing Davids. Young erotic Davids. Fashioned in our father's image' (p. 115). Oscar has become 'Jewish' even though it is this mistress who knows Oscar's secret. His mistress 'was the only one who really saw that Oscar was not Oscar, smelled his bastard genes, the oily stench of his "coolie" ancestry' (p. 112). In becoming a Jew he also becomes one whose success marks him as only superficially 'white'. Oscar's therapist, Amina Mandelstam, notes that 'the name he took – Oscar – defined his personality' (p. 47). It made him into a Jew. It also defined his body, as it did Amina's husband. Her husband was Jewish: 'The cripple Jew was being questioned [about Oscar's death]. But there was no photo of him. I wonder what a cripple Jew looks like?', asks one of his relatives (p. 103). The 'Jew' is defined by his crippled (circumcised body), but it is also simultaneously the body of the Muslim man.

Hybridity is the centrepiece of this magic realist tale in which the protagonist eventually develops symptoms of an unknown disease, Kafka's curse, which transforms him virtually into a tree, breathing carbon dioxide and expelling oxygen. As with Kafka it is the fantasy of Jewish physical difference that defines the Jew, no matter whether he is 'Jewish' or not. Like Coleman Silk, the protagonist of Roth's *The Human Stain*, Oscar becomes a Jew and therefore adapts all of the perceived physical differences of the Jew. The society here, that of apartheid South Africa, roots its image of the Jew in the discourse of a false cosmopolitanism that is merely the world of the 'Oriental', here again defined as the Eastern Jew, the Litvak, in a Western society. Dangor's image of apartheid South Africa evokes the world of Nazi Germany with all the anxiety about passing. Writing from a post-apartheid perspective, Dangor can present the image of the Jew into which his protagonist has transformed himself in the most ironic manner. Yet it is also clear that Dangor's reading of this transformation, with its overt reference to the transformation of Gregor Samsa, is that it is a failure because of its very necessity.

Transformation in upstate New York takes on quite a different meaning than it does in Philip Roth's world. Lecturing to undergraduates in his world literature course at Cornell University 50 years after Kafka's death, Vladimir Nabokov, himself a renowned lepidopterist, provides a detailed reading of this 'entomological fantasy'. Part of the authenticity of Nabokov's reading is his own claim that he had lived near Kafka in Berlin in the 1920s. Nabokov's reading is original in every way but also reveals his own desires for Samsa and for Kafka:

Commentators say [that Samsa is a] cockroach, which of course does not make sense. A cockroach is an insect that is flat in shape with large legs, and Gregor is anything but flat: he is convex on both sides, belly and back, and his legs are small. He approaches a cockroach in only one respect: his coloration is brown. That is all. Apart from this he has a tremendous convex belly divided into segments and a hard rounded back suggestive of wing cases. In beetles these cases conceal flimsy little wings that can be expanded and then may carry the beetle for miles and miles in a blundering flight. Curiously enough, Gregor the beetle never found out that he had wings under the hard covering of his back. (This is a very nice observation on my part to be treasured all your lives. Some Gregors, some Joes and Janes, do not know that they have wings.)

Had Samsa but known that he could fly? Nabokov's elite undergraduates now know he could have left the Samsa family apartment and become a . . . What could he have become? How flexible is the real world, the world of Joes and Janes, for huge flying insects that think. Certainly transformation of the scientist Andre Delambre (played by David Hedison) into *The Fly* (dir. Kurt Neumann, 1958) is not exactly accepted into the world of Joes and Janes. Popular film was, however, a medium to transform Kafka into a 'contemporary'.

Kafka's world was a visual world even though (or exactly because) it was one that could not be represented. Remember, Kafka refused to allow his publisher to put a picture of Gregor Samsa on the cover of *The Metamorphosis*. Still Kafka became the inspiration for myriad films. Certainly the most important is Orson Welles's 1962 Francophone version of *The Trial*, starring Anthony Perkins as Josef K., Romy Schneider as Leni, Jeanne Moreau as Miss Bürstner and Welles himself as Dr Hasterer (the Advocate). The film was generally poorly reviewed when it first appeared. It has, however, become part of the film canon always evoked when the question of translating the verbal into the visual is studied.

Welles rewrote and reordered the text. His dialogue remade the world of Prague into the world of the Cold War, as two exchanges about guilt and life at the very beginning of the film show:

Josef K.: It's never any use, is it, apologizing. It's even worse when you haven't done anything wrong and you still feel guilty. I can remember my father looking at me, you know, straight in the eye: 'Come on, boy,' he'd say, 'exactly what have you been up to?' And even when I hadn't been up to anything at all I'd still feel guilty – you know that feeling? And the teacher at school making the announcement that she was missing something from her desk: 'All right, who's the guilty one?' It was me, of course. I'd feel just sick with guilt – and I didn't even know what was missing. Maybe – yeah, that must be it – unless your thoughts are innocent, one hundred percent. Can that be said of anybody? Even the saints have temptations . . . [kisses Miss Burstner]. What do you think?

Miss Bürstner: I think you're crazy.

Miss Bürstner: What's your problem?

Josef K.: I'm under arrest.

Miss Bürstner: Yeah?

Josef K.: Unbelievable, isn't it?

Miss Bürstner: Well, it happens.

Josef K.: Well, that's just the point? I don't know how it happened. I haven't the remotest idea.

Miss Bürstner: How do you know you're arrested? It isn't something you just suddenly notice like bleeding gums.

Welles's references are as much to a world caught between two conflicting ideologies and damaged by this tension. With the sense that one is guilty even (or especially) when one does nothing being reinforced by the show trials under and after Stalin, and by Joseph McCarthy's 'Red Scare' and its Cold War aftermath, Welles's cinematic message was clear. This was certainly not a message that would have made for a popular success and it did not.

Yet Welles also found it necessary to change the ending. Kafka was not American enough in providing an open ending to resolve the puzzle of K.'s trial. Like Roth's later vision of a Jewish Kafka, Welles needed a Kafka that allowed for hope and transcendence. Welles wrote that

> I couldn't put my name to a work that implies man's ultimate surrender. Being on the side of man, I had to show him in his final hour undefeated . . . I do not share Kafka's point of view in *The Trial*. I believe that he is a good writer, but Kafka is not the extraordinary genius that people today see in him. He [Joseph K.] is a little bureaucrat. I consider him guilty . . . He belongs to a guilty society; he collaborates with it. What made it possible for me to make the picture is that I've had recurring nightmares of guilt all my life: I'm in prison and I don't know why – going to be tried and I don't know why. It's very personal for me. A very personal experience, and it's not at all true that I'm off in some foreign world that has no application to myself; it's the most autobiographical movie that I've ever made, the only one that's really close to me. And just because it doesn't speak in a Middle West accent doesn't mean a damn thing. It's much closer to my own feelings about everything than any other picture I've ever made.

Anthony Perkins, Welles's but not Kafka's Joseph K., found this reading quite different from his sense of the book:

> I think the movie [*The Trial*] is a bit of a mess . . . The concept of a guilty Joseph K., a sort of obsequious and weak hero, seemed very antithetical to the spirit of Kafka's book. After a couple of days of shooting I said to Orson [Welles], 'Don't you think it's going to be interpreted that K. is guilty?' He said, 'He is guilty! He's guilty as hell!' And I thought, 'Oh, well, okay.' I believed then, as I do now, in the authenticity of the director's vision,

and I'll do anything to make it come true.'

Thus the American and then the world audience was treated to a happy end; one quite in keeping with Kafka's experience of the Yiddish theatre in Prague with its version of *King Lear* ending with the reconciliation of the family.

The world of the film was haunted by Kafka, but so was the world of high art. Poets used and use Kafka as a sign for virtually everything. The Beat poets saw him through Camus as the modern, alienated self. Lawrence Ferlinghetti (1919–), in the exemplary beat volume *A Coney Island of the Mind* (1958), sees the world from Kafka's perspective:

> Kafka's Castle stands above the world
>
> like a last bastille
>
> of the Mystery of Existence
>
> Its blind approaches baffle us
>
> Steep paths
>
> plunge nowhere from it
>
> Roads radiate into air
>
> like the labyrinth wires
>
> of a telephone central
>
> thru which all calls are
>
> infinitely untraceable
>
> Up there
>
> it is heavenly weather
>
> Souls dance undressed

                                  together

                        and like loiterers

                                  on the fringes of a fair

                  we ogle the unobtainable

                                  imagined mystery

                  Yet away around on the far side

                                  like the stage door of a circus tent

                  is a wide wide vent in the battlements

                                  where even elephants

                                          waltz thru

In Britain, Ted Hughes (1930–1998), in *Wodwo* (1967), sang of
another Kafka:

Kafka

And he is an owl
He is an owl, 'Man' tattooed in his armpit
Under the broken wing
[Stunned by the wall of glare, he fell here]
Under the broken wing of huge shadow that twitches across
    the floor.
He is a man in hopeless feathers.

At the same moment, across the Atlantic, Delmore Schwartz
(1913–1966) concluded his last, great poem on 'Seurat's Sunday
Afternoon along the Seine' with the saddest thought that

The kingdom of heaven on earth on Sunday summer day.
Is it not clear and clearer? Can we not also hear

The voice of Kafka, forever sad, in despair's sickness trying
    to say
'Flaubert was right: *Ils sont dans le vrai*!
Without forbears, without marriage, without heirs,
Yet with a wild longing for forbears, marriage, and heirs:
They all stretch out their hands to me: but they are too
    far away!'

Kafka as the writer without peer in his suffering and yet, as Roth implies, even Schwartz becomes his heir.

Each of the poets can evoke their own private Kafka and yet evoke at the very same instance the world that was his own. Kafka becomes one of the pegs onto which the modern age is hung. So much so that it echoes even until the end of the millennium and beyond, as Stephen Dunn (1939–) ironically gestures at the Centre Georges Pompidou 1984 exhibition of Central European culture that canonized Kafka as the high priest of this Kafkaesque age:

Sometimes I'd rather be ankle-deep
    in mud puddles,
        swatting flies with the Holsteins,
I'd rather be related to that punky boy
    with purple hair
        walking toward the antique shop
            than talk with someone who doesn't know
he lives
    in '*Le Siècle de Kafka*,' as the French
        dubbed it in 1984.

But now we all know it.

References

1 My Family and my Body as a Curse

1 Quoted by Sander L. Gilman, *Franz Kafka: The Jewish Patient* (New York, 1995), p. 10.
2 Franz Kafka, *The Diaries, 1914–1923*, ed. Max Brod, trans. Martin Greenberg and Hannah Arendt (New York, 1949), pp. 73–4.
3 *Ibid.*, p. 160.
4 Franz Kafka, 'Letter to the Father', trans. Ernst Kaiser and Eithne Wilkens, revised by Arthur S. Wensinger, in Franz Kafka, *The Sons*, intro. Mark Anderson (New York, 1989), p. 117.
5 Fritz Mauthner, *Erinnerungen. 1. Prager Jugendjahre* (Munich, 1918), pp. 52–3.
6 Franz Kafka, *Letters to Milena*, trans. Philip Boehm (New York, 1990), p. 59.
7 Franz Kafka, *Letters to Felice*, ed. Erich Heller and Jürgen Born, trans. James Stern and Elisabeth Duckworth (New York, 1973), p. 113.
8 Franz Kafka, *The Diaries, 1914–1923*, p. 11.
9 Franz Kafka, *Letters to Milena*, p. 198.
10 Franz Kafka, *Letters to Felice*, p. 27.
11 *Ibid.*, p. 254.
12 Franz Kafka, *The Diaries, 1914–1923*, p. 24.
13 *Ibid.*, p. 11.
14 Franz Kafka, 'Letter to the Father', p. 136.
15 Franz Kafka, *Letters to Friends, Family, and Editors*, ed. Max Brod, trans. Richard and Clara Winston (New York, 1977), p. 89.
16 *Ibid.*, p. 67.
17 Franz Kafka, *The Diaries, 1910–1913*, p. 60.
18 Franz Kafka, *Letters to Felice*, p. 208.

2 Writing

1 Franz Kafka, *The Complete Stories*, ed. Nahum N. Glatzer (New York, 1971), p. 77.
2 Franz Kafka, *The Complete Stories*, p. 87.
3 *Ibid.*, p. 85.
4 *Ibid.*, p. 85.

5 *Ibid.*, p. 390.

6 Franz Kafka, *Letters to Felice*, p. 134.

7 Franz Kafka, *The Complete Stories*, pp. 394–5.

8 Franz Kafka, *The Diaries, 1910–1913*, p. 181.

9 *Ibid.*, p. 298.

10 Franz Kafka, *Amerika: The Man Who Disappeared*, trans. Michael Hofman (New York, 1996), p. 3.

11 *Ibid.*, p. 32.

12 *Ibid.*, p. 89.

13 Franz Kafka, *Letters to Milena*, p. 136.

14 Franz Kafka, *Letters to Felice*, p. 270.

15 Franz Kafka, *Letters to Friends, Family, and Editors*, p. 334.

16 Franz Kafka, *The Diaries, 1910–1913*, p. 301.

17 Franz Kafka, *Letters to Felice*, p. 334.

18 Franz Kafka, *The Diaries, 1910–1913*, p. 305.

19 *Ibid.*, p. 309.

20 Franz Kafka, *Letters to Felice*, p. 352.

21 *Ibid.*, p. 293.

22 *Ibid.*, p. 434.

23 Franz Kafka, *The Diaries, 1914–1923*, p. 153.

24 Franz Kafka, *Letters to Friends, Family, and Editors*, p. 237.

25 Franz Kafka, *The Complete Stories*, p. 81.

26 *Ibid.*, p. 85.

27 Franz Kafka, 'Letter to the Father', p. 120.

28 Franz Kafka, *Letters to Ottla and the Family*, trans. Richard and Clara Winston, ed. N. N. Glatzer (New York, 1982), p. 9.

29 Franz Kafka, *The Complete Stories*, p. 140.

30 *Ibid.*, p. 163.

31 *Ibid.*, p. 146.

32 Franz Kafka, *The Trial*, trans. Breon Mitchell (New York, 1998), p. 3.

33 *Ibid.*, pp. 215–17.

34 *Ibid.*, p. 231.

35 *Ibid.*, p. 6.

36 *Ibid.*, p. 1.

37 Franz Kafka, *Letters to Friends, Family, and Editors*, pp. 286–9 [p. 289].

38 Franz Kafka, *Letters to Felice*, p. 57.

39 *Ibid.*, p. 78.

40 Franz Kafka, *The Complete Stories*, p. 89.

41 *Ibid.*, p. 89.

42 *Ibid.*, p. 118.

43 *Ibid.*, p. 133.

44 *Ibid.*, p. 136.

45 *Ibid.*, p. 139.

46 Franz Kafka, *Letters to Felice*, p. 425.

47 Franz Kafka, *Letters to Friends, Family, and Editors*, p. 339.

48 Franz Kafka, *Letters to Felice*, p. 543.

49 Franz Kafka, *The Diaries, 1914–1923*, p. 182.

50 Franz Kafka, *Letters to Felice*, p. 544.

3 A Life ill

1 Franz Kafka, *The Diaries, 1914–1923*, p. 322.

2 Franz Kafka, *The Complete Stories*, p. 122.

3 *Ibid.*, p. 221.

4 *Ibid.*, p. 223.

5 *Ibid.*, p. 223.

6 *Ibid.*, p. 224.

7 Franz Kafka, *The Diaries, 1914–1923*, p. 140.

8 Franz Kafka, *Letters to Friends, Family, and Editors*, p. 213.

9 Franz Kafka, *Letters to Milena*, p. 223.

10 *Ibid.*, p. 37.

11 *Ibid.*, p. 136.

12 *Ibid.*, p. 144.

13 *Ibid.*, p. 202.

14 Franz Kafka, *The Complete Stories*, p. 268.

15 *Ibid.*, p. 277.

16 Franz Kafka, *The Diaries, 1914–1923*, p. 225.

17 *Ibid.*, pp. 230–31.

18 Franz Kafka, *Letters to Friends, Family, and Editors*, p. 330.

19 Hans Blüher, *Secessio Judaica: Philosophische Grundlegung der historischen Situation des Judenthums und der antisemitischen Bewegung* (Berlin, 1922), p. 19.

20 Werner Sombart, *The Jews and Modern Capitalism*, trans. M. Epstein (Glencoe, IL, 1951), p. 272.

21 Blüher, p. 23.

22 *Ibid.*, p. 25.

23 Franz Kafka, *Letters to Friends, Family, and Editors*, p. 373.

24 *Ibid.*, p. 372.

25 *Ibid.*, p. 372.

26 Max Brod, 'Brief an eine Schülerin nach Galizien', *Der Jude*, I (1916–17), pp. 124–5.

27 *Ibid.*, pp. 380-81.

28 Franz Kafka, *Letters to Ottla and the Family*, p. 77.

29 Franz Kafka, *The Complete Stories*, p. 328.

30 *Ibid.*, p. 341.

31 *Ibid.*, p. 340.

32 Franz Kafka, *Letters to Friends, Family, and Editors*, p. 264.

Bibliography and Filmography

1 Editions

There are two new competing editions in progress of the German texts of Kafka: the facsimile *Historisch-kritische Ausgabe sämtlicher Handschriften, Drucke und Typoskripte*, edited by Roland Reuss and Peter Staengle and published from 1995 by Stroemfeld in Basel; and the critical *Schriften, Tagebücher, Briefe: kritische Ausgabe*, edited by Jost Schillemeit and Malcolm Pasley and published by Fischer in Frankfurt, beginning in 1982. Both are incomplete at present. The six volumes of Max Brod's highly subjective edition, *Gesammelte Werke*, I–IV (ed. Max Brod and Heinz Politzer, Berlin: Schocken, 1935–7); V–VI (ed. Max Brod, Prague: Heinr. Mercy Sohn), served as the basis for all of the translations and criticism up to the 1990s.

2 Standard English translations

The Trial, trans. Breon Mitchell (New York, 1998)
The Complete Stories, ed. Nahum N. Glatzer (New York, 1971)
The Castle, trans. Mark Harman (New York, 1998)
Amerika: The Man Who Disappeared, trans. Michael Hofman (New York, 1996)
Parables and Paradoxes (New York, 1963)
'Letter to the Father', trans. Ernst Kaiser and Eithne Wilkens, revd Arthur S.
    Wensinger, in Franz Kafka, *The Sons*, intro. Mark Anderson (New York, 1989)
The Diaries, 1910–1913, ed. Max Brod, trans. Joseph Kresh (New York, 1948)
The Diaries, 1914–1923, ed. Max Brod, trans. Martin Greenberg and Hannah Arendt
    (New York, 1949)
Letters to Friends, Family, and Editors, ed. Max Brod, trans. Richard and Clara Winston
    (New York, 1977)
Letters to Felice, ed. Erich Heller and Jürgen Born, trans. James Stern and Elisabeth
    Duckworth (New York, 1973)
Letters to Milena, trans. Philip Boehm (New York, 1990)
Letters to Ottla and the Family, ed. N. N. Glatzer, trans. Richard and Clara Winston
    (New York, 1982)

3 Bibliographies

The following bibliographies may suggest the scale of the 'Kafka-Industry' foretold by Hannah Arendt:

Beicken, Peter, *Franz Kafka: Eine kritische Einführung in die Forschung* (Frankfurt am Main, 1974)

Binder, Hartmut, ed., *Kafka: Handbuch in zwei Bänden*, 2 vols (Stuttgart, 1979)

——, *Kafka: Kommentar zu den Romanen, Rezensionen, Aphorismen und zum Brief an den Vater* (Munich, 1976)

——, *Kafka: Kommentar zu sämtlichen Erzählungen* (Munich, 1982)

Caputo-Mayr, Maria Luise, *Franz Kafka: eine kommentierte Bibliographie der Sekundärliteratur (1955–1980, mit einem Nachtrag 1985)* (Bern, 1987)

——, *Franz Kafka: internationale Bibliographie der Primär- und Sekundärliteratur: eine Einführung*, 3rd edn (Munich, 2000)

——, *Franz Kafkas Werke: eine Bibliographie der Primärliteratur (1908–1980)* (Bern, 1982)

Corngold, Stanley, *The Commentators' Despair: The Interpretation of Kafka's 'Metamorphosis'* (Port Washington, NY, 1973)

Dietz, Ludwig, *Franz Kafka*, 2nd edn, Sammlung Metzler, vol. 138 (Stuttgart, 1990)

——, *Franz Kafka: die Veröffentlichungen zu seinen Lebzeiten (1908–1924): eine textkritische und kommentierte Bibliographie* (Heidelberg, 1982)

Flores, Angel, ed., *The Kafka Problem* (New York, [1946], repr. 1975)

——, *The Kafka Problem: With a New, Up-to-Date Bibliography & a Complete List of Kafka's Works in English* (New York, 1963)

Flores, Angel, *A Kafka Bibliography, 1908–1976* (New York, 1976)

Preece, Julian, ed., *The Cambridge Companion to Kafka* (Cambridge, 2002)

Rieck, Gerhard, *Franz Kafka und die Literaturwissenschaft: Aufsätze zu einem kafkaesken Verhältnis* (Würzburg, 2002)

Robertson, Ritchie, 'In Search of the Historical Kafka: A Selective Review of Research, 1980–92', *Modern Language Review*, 89 (1994), pp. 107–37

Rolleston, James, ed., *A Companion to the Works of Franz Kafka* (Rochester, NY, 2002)

Tabéry, Françoise, *Kafka en France: essai de bibliographie annotée* (Paris, 1991)

4 Kafka's library

Born, Jürgen, ed., *Kafkas Bibliothek: ein beschreibendes Verzeichnis mit einem Index aller in Kafkas Schriften erwähnten Bücher, Zeitschriften und Zeitschriftenbeitrage; zusammengestellt unter Mitarbeit von Michael Antreter, Waltraud John und Jon Shepherd* (Frankfurt am Main, 1991)

5 Kafka's life and times

Adler, Jeremy, *Franz Kafka* (London and New York, 2001)
Anderson, Mark, *Kafka's Clothes: Ornament and Aestheticism in the Habsburg Fin de Siècle* (Oxford, 1992)
Anderson, Mark, ed., *Reading Kafka: Prague, Politics, and the Fin de Siècle* (New York, 1989)
Bezzel, Christoph, *Kafka-Chronik: [Daten zu Leben u. Werk]* (Munich and Vienna, 1975)
Binder, Hartmut, *Franz Kafka: Leben und Personlichkeit* (Stuttgart, [1983])
——, *Kafka, ein Leben in Prag* (Munich, 1982)
Bergman, Schmuel Hugo, *Tagebücher und Briefe*, ed. Miriam Sambursky, 2 vols (Frankfurt am Main, 1985)
Bloom, Harold, *The Strong Light of the Canonical: Kafka, Freud and Scholem as Revisionists of Jewish Culture and Thought* (New York, 1987)
Boa, Elizabeth, *Kafka: Gender, Class and Race in the Letters and Fictions* (Oxford, 1996)
Brenner, David, 'Uncovering the Father: Kafka, Judaism, and Homoeroticism', in *Kafka, Zionism, and* Beyond, ed. Mark Gelber (Tübingen, 2004), pp. 207–18
Brod, Max, *Franz Kafka, A Biography*, 2nd edn, trans. G. Humphreys Roberts and Richard Winston (New York, [1960])
Brod, Max, and Hans-Joachim Schoeps, *Im Streit um Kafka und das Judentum: Max Brod Hans-Joachim Schoeps Briefwechsel* (Königstein im Taunus, 1985)
Buber-Neumann, Margarete, *Mistress to Kafka: The Life and Death of Milena* (London, 1966)
Camp, Hélène van, *En deuil de Franz Kafka* (Paris, 1996)
Canetti, Elias, *Kafka's Other Trial: The Letters to Felice* (New York, 1974)
Cerna, Jana, *Kafka's Milena* (London, 1988)
Citati, Pietro, *Kafka*, trans. Raymond Rosenthal (London, 1990)
Coots, Steve, *Kafka* (London, 2002)
Demetz, Peter, *The Air Show at Brescia, 1909* (New York, 2002)
Diamant, Kathi, *Kafka's Last Love: The Mystery of Dora Diamant* (New York, 2003)
Eichenhofer, Eberhard, *Franz Kafka und die Sozialversicherung* (Stuttgart, 1997)
Fertig, Ludwig, *Abends auf den Helikon: Dichter und ihre Berufe von Lessing bis Kafka* (Darmstadt, 1996)
Gilman, Sander L., 'A View of Kafka's Treatment of Actuality in *Die Verwandlung*', *Germanic Notes*, 2 (1971), pp. 26–30
——, 'Kafka Wept', *Modernism/Modernity*, 1 (1994), pp. 17–37
——, 'Dreyfusens Körper – Kafkas Angst', in *Dreyfus und die Folgen*, ed. Julius H. Schoeps and Hermann Simon (Berlin, 1995), pp. 212–33
——, 'Damaged Men: Thoughts on Kafka's Body', in *Constructing Masculinity*, ed. Maurice Berger, Brian Wallis and Simon Watson (New York, 1995), pp. 176–92
——, *Franz Kafka: The Jewish Patient* (New York, 1995)
——, 'Kafka's "Papa"', in *Paternity and Fatherhood*, ed. Lieve Spaas (London, 1998), pp. 175–85
——, 'Zeugenschaft und jüdische Männlichkeit," in *Einstein Forum: Jahrbuch – Zeugnis*

und Zeugenschaft, 1 (1999), pp. 157–79

——, 'A Dream of Jewishness Denied: Kafka's Tumor and 'Ein Landarzt', in *A Companion to the Works of Franz Kafka*, ed. James Rolleston (Rochester, NY, 2002), pp. 263–80

Greenberg, Valerie D., *Transgressive Readings: The Texts of Franz Kafka and Max Planck* (Ann Arbor, 1990)

Grözinger, Karl Erich, Stéphane Mosès and Hans Dieter Zimmermann, eds, *Kafka und das Judentum* (Frankfurt am Main, 1987)

Grözinger, Karl Erich, *Kafka and Kabbalah*, trans. Susan Hecker Ray (New York, 1994)

Gruša, Jiří, *Franz Kafka of Prague*, trans. Eric Mosbacher (London, 1983)

Hackermüller, Rotraut, *Das Leben, das mich stört: eine Dokumentation zu Kafkas letzten Jahren 1917–1924* (Vienna, 1984, repr. Munich, 1990)

Hayman, Ronald, *Kafka: A Biography* (New York, 1982)

Henisch, Peter, *Vom Wunsch, Indianer zu werden: wie Franz Kafka Karl May traf und trotzdem nicht in Amerika landete* (Salzburg, 1994)

Hockaday, Mary, *Kafka, Love and Courage: The Life of Milena Jesenska* (London, 1995)

Hoffman, N. Y., 'Franz Kafka – His Father's Son: A Study in Literary Sexuality', *Journal of the American Medical Association*, CCXXIX (1974), pp. 1623–6

Janouch, Gustav, *Gespräche mit Kafka: Aufzeichnungen und Erinnerungen* (Frankfurt am Main, 1981)

——, *Conversations with Kafka*, trans. Goronwy Rees, 2nd edn (New York, [1971])

Jofen, Jean, *The Jewish Mystic in Kafka* (New York, 1987)

Karl, Frederick Robert, *Franz Kafka, Representative Man* (New York, 1991)

Kafka, Franz, *Briefe an die Eltern aus den Jahren 1922–1924* (Prague, 1990)

Koch, Hans-Gerd, ed., *'Als Kafka mir entgegenkam . . . ': Erinnerungen an Franz Kafka* (Berlin, 1995)

Kurz, Gerhard, ed., *Der Junge Kafka* (Frankfurt am Main, 1984)

Lensing, Leo A., 'Franz would be with us here: The Posthumous Papers of Robert Klopstock', *Times Literary Supplement* (28 Feb 2003), pp. 13–15

Loeb, Sara, *Franz Kafka: A Question of Jewish Identity: Two Perspectives*, trans. Sondra Silverston and Chaya Naor (Lanham, MD, 2001)

Mailloux, Peter Alden, *A Hesitation before Birth: The Life of Franz Kafka* (Newark, DE, 1989)

Mairowitz, David Zane, *Introducing Kafka*, illus. Robert Crumb, ed. Richard Appignanesi (Duxford, 2000)

Müller-Seidel, Walter, *Die Deportation des Menschen: Kafkas Erzählung 'In der Strafkolonie' im europäischen Kontext* (Stuttgart, 1986)

Murray, Nicholas, *Kafka* (London, 2004)

Nabokov, Vladimir, *Lectures on Literature*, ed. Fredson Bowers (London, 1983)

Neesen, Peter, *Vom Louvrezirkel zum Prozess: Franz Kafka und die Psychologie Franz Brentanos* (Göppingen, 1972)

Northey, Anthony, *Kafkas Mischpoche* (Berlin, 1988)

——, *Kafka's Relatives: Their Lives and his Writing* (New Haven, CT, 1991)

Pappenheim, Bertha [Anna O.], *Literarische and Publizistische Texts*, ed. Lena Kugler and Albrecht Koschorke (Vienna, 2002)

Pawel, Ernst, *The Nightmare of Reason: A Life of Franz Kafka* (New York, 1984)

Politzer, Heinz, *Franz Kafka: Parable and Paradox*, rev. edn (Ithaca, NY, 1966)

Robert, Marthe, *As Lonely as Franz Kafka*, trans. Ralph Manheim (New York, 1986)

Robertson, Ritchie, *Kafka: Judaism, Politics, and Literature* (Oxford, 1985)

Robin, Régine, *Kafka* (Paris, 1989)

Salfellner, Harald, *Franz Kafka und Prag* (Prague, 1998)

Sharp, Daryl, *The Secret Raven: Conflict and Transformation in the Life of Franz Kafka* (Toronto, 1980)

Sokel, Walter H., *The Myth of Power and the Self: Essays on Franz Kafka* (Detroit, 2002)

Spector, Scott, *Prague Territories: National Conflict and Cultural Innovation in Franz Kafka's fin de siècle* (Berkeley, CA, 2000)

Stach, Reiner, *Kafka: Die Jahre der Entscheidungen* (Frankfurt, 2002); review by Sander L. Gilman in *Literaturen* (Jan 2003), pp. 12–20

Stölzl, Christoph, *Kafkas böses Bohmen: zur Sozialgeschichte eines Prager Juden* (Frankfurt am Main, 1989)

Sudaka-Benazeraf, Jacqueline, *Le regard de Franz Kafka: dessins d'un écrivain* (Paris, 2001)

Unseld, Joachim, *Franz Kafka, ein Schriftstellerleben: die Geschichte seiner Veröffentlichungen mit einer Bibliographie sämtlicher Drucke und Ausgaben der Dichtungen Franz Kafkas, 1908–1924* (Munich, 1982)

Wagenbach, Klaus, *Franz Kafka in Selbstzeugnissen und Bilddokumenten* (Reinbek bei Hamburg, 1964)

——, *Franz Kafka: Eine Biographie seiner Jugend* (Bern, 1958)

——, *Kafka*, trans. Ewald Osers (Cambridge, MA, 2003)

Wagnerova, Alena K., *Milena Jesenska: Biographie* (Mannheim, 1994)

Werckmeister, Otto Karl, *Icons of the Left: Benjamin and Eisenstein, Picasso and Kafka after the Fall of Communism* (Chicago, 1999)

Wetscherek, Hugo, ed., *Kafkas letzter Freund: der Nachlass Robert Klopstock (1899–1972), mit kommentierter Erstveröffentlichung von 38 teils ungedruckten Briefen Franz Kafkas* (Vienna, 2003)

Wood, Michael, *Franz Kafka* (Tavistock, 2003)

Zilcosky, John, *Kafka's Travels: Exoticism, Colonialism, and the Traffic of Writing* (New York, 2003)

Zischler, Hanns, *Kafka Goes to the Movies*, trans. Susan H. Gillespie (Chicago, 2003)

6 Filmography

[*The Trial*]: *Der Prozeß* (Austria: dir. Georg Wilhelm Pabst, 1948), with Max Brod as the Judensprecher

['A Report for an Academy']: *Ein Bericht für eine Akademie* (West Germany: dir. Willi Schmidt for the Berliner Akademie der Künste, 1963), with Klaus Kammer as Rotpeter

[*The Trial*]: *Le procès* (France/Germany/Italy: dir. Orson Welles, 1963), with Anthony Perkins as Joseph K

['The Warden of the Tomb']: *De Grafbewaker* (Netherlands: dir. Harry Kümel, 1965), with Josée Bernaus, Jef Demedts, Werner Kopers, Julien Schoenaerts, Frans Vandenbrande, Theo Op de Beeck

[*The Castle*]: *Das Schloß* (West Germany: dir. Rudolf Noelte, 1968), with Maximilian Schell as 'K'

['The Penal Colony']: *La colonia penal* (Chile: dir. Raúl Ruiz, 1970), with Luis Alarcón, Mónica Echeverría, Anibal Reyna, Nelson Villagra

['The Metamorphosis']: *Metamorphosis* (Czechoslovakia: dir. Jan Němec, 1975) shot from the perspective of Gregor Samsa, no actors

['The Metamorphosis']: *Förvandlingen* (Sweden: dir. Ivo Dvořák, 1976), with Peter Schildt as Gregor Samsa

['A Fratricide']: *Bratrovrazda* (Czechoslovakia: dir. Miroslav Janek, 1977)

The Metamorphosis of Mr. Samsa (Canada: dir. Caroline Leaf, 1977) [animated short]

[*Amerika*]: *Klassenverhältnisse* (France/West Germany: dir. Jean-Marie Straub and Danièle Huillet, 1984), with Christian Heinisch as Karl Rossmann

[*The Castle*]: *Linna* (Finnish: dir. Jaakko Pakkasvirta, 1986) with Carl-Kristian Rundman as The Surveyor

Metamorphosis (UK: dir. Jim Goddard, screenplay Steven Berkoff, 1987), with Tim Roth as Gregor Samsa and Steven Berkoff as Mr Samsa [TV film of Berkoff's 1981 play]

Los Amores de Kafka (Argentina: dir. Beda Docampo Feijóo, 1988), with Jorge Marrale as Franz Kafka

Vladimir Nabokov on Kafka: Understanding 'The Metamorphosis' (UK: dir. Peter Medak, 1990), with Christopher Plummer as Nabokov

Kafka (UK: dir. Steven Soderbergh, 1991), with Jeremy Irons as Kafka

The Trial (UK: dir. David Hugh Jones, screenplay Harold Pinter, 1993), with Kyle MacLachlan as Josef K. and Anthony Hopkins as The Priest

Franz Kafka's It's a Wonderful Life (UK: dir. and screenplay Peter Capaldi, 1993), with Richard E. Grant as Franz Kafka and Crispin Letts as Gregor Samsa

['Josephine, the Singer']: *Spivachka Zhosefina i myshachyj narod* (Ukraine: dir. Sergei Maslobojshchikov, 1994)

Amerika (Czechoslovakia: dir. Vladimír Michálek, 1994), with Martin Dejdar as Karel Rossman

[*The Castle*]: *Zamok* (Russia: dir. Aleksei Balabanov, 1994), with Nikolai Stotsky as the Land Surveyor

[*The Castle*]: *Das Schloß* (Austria/Germany: dir. Michael Haneke, 1997), with Ulrich Mühe as K. [TV film]

The Sickroom (Canada: dir. Serge Marcotte, 1998)

K.af.ka Fragment (Germany: dir. Christian Frosch, 2001) with Lars Rudolf as Kafka and Ursula Ofner as Felice Bauer (TV).

Kafka va au cinéma (France/Germany: dir. Hanns Zischler, 2002) [TV documentary based on his book of the same name]

On the films

Adams, Jeffrey, 'Orson Welles's *The Trial: film noir* and the Kafkaesque', *College Literature*, 29 (2002), pp. 140–57

Marks, Louis, 'Producing *The Trial*: a Personal Memoir', in *The Films of Harold Pinter*, ed. Steven H. Gale (Albany, NY, 2001), pp. 109–21

Peucker, Brigitte, 'Kubrick and Kafka: the Corporeal Uncanny', *Modernism/Modernity*, VIII (2001), pp. 663–74

Acknowledgements

The author and publishers wish to express their grateful thanks to Archiv Klaus Wagenbach, who supplied all the picture material used in this book; all images are © Archiv Klaus Wagenbach.

Permissions for quotations are as follows: 'Smiles', from *New and Selected Poems, 1974–1994* by Stephen Dunn. Copyright © 1994 by Stephen Dunn. Used by permission of W. W. Norton & Company, Inc. 'Kafka's Castle #16', by Lawrence Ferlinghetti, from *A Coney Island of the Mind*, copyright © 1958 by Lawrence Ferlinghetti. Reprinted by permission of New Directions Publishing Corp. Miroslav Holub, *Poems Before & After: Collected English Translations*, eds. Ian & Jarmila Milner, Ewald Osers, George Theiner (Bloodaxe Books, 1990). Lines from 'Wings', Part II; 'Kafka', from Ted Hughes, *Wodwo*, © 1967 by Ted Hughes. Reprinted by permission of Faber & Faber Ltd, London. 'Seurat's Sunday Afternoon Along the Seine', by Delmore Schwartz, from *Selected Poems: Summer Knowledge*, copyright © 1959 by Delmore Schwartz. Reprinted by permission of New Directions Publishing Corp. Lines from 'Tea at the Palaz of Hoon', from Wallace Stevens, *Collected Poems of Wallace Stevens*, © Wallace Stevens. Reprinted by permission of Faber & Faber Ltd, London.